P9-CNH-829

No Room at the Table

Earth's Most Vulnerable Children

DONALD H. DUNSON

ORBIS BOOKS
Maryknoll, New York 10545

Founded in 1970, Orbis Books endeavors to publish works that enlighten the mind, nourish the spirit, and challenge the conscience. The publishing arm of the Maryknoll Fathers and Brothers, Orbis seeks to explore the global dimensions of the Christian faith and mission, to invite dialogue with diverse cultures and religious traditions, and to serve the cause of reconciliation and peace. The books published reflect the views of their authors and do not represent the official position of the Maryknoll Society. To learn more about Maryknoll and Orbis Books, please visit our website at www.maryknoll.org.

Copyright © 2003 by Donald H. Dunson

Published by Orbis Books, Maryknoll, New York 10545-0308.
Manufactured in the United States of America.

All rights reserved. No part of this publication may be reproduced or transmitted in any form or by any means, electronic or mechanical, including photocopying, recording or any information storage or retrieval system, without prior permission in writing from the publisher.

Queries regarding rights and permissions should be addressed to: Orbis Books, P.O. Box 308, Maryknoll, New York 10545-0308.

Library of Congress Cataloging-in-Publication Data

Dunson, Donald H.
  No room at the table / Donald H. Dunson.
     p. cm.
  ISBN 1-57075-491-8 (pbk.)
  1. Children—Social conditions. I. Title.
  HQ781 .D73 2003
  305.23—dc21
                                              2003009825

Contents

iv   Contents

Foreword

can vividly remember the summer day in 2001 when I first welcomed a visiting American priest to my home. He was Donald Dunson, a moral theologian and seminary professor from the diocese of Cleveland, Ohio. For many years, Father Dunson's pastoral mission had highlighted the plight of exploited, abused, and abandoned children. Indeed, the urgent needs of the world's children had brought him here to Uganda. For his sabbatical semester, he had traveled eight thousand miles to live with us, to learn from us, and to be in solidarity with us. He wanted to research the stories of the vulnerable children of East Central Africa. He wanted to see how it might be possible for them and for us to transform their suffering into redemptive action. This book is an eloquent expression of the thoughts and experiences that came together while he was with us.

In the region of my archdiocese of Gulu, in Uganda, violence and disease have devastated the lives of thousands of children. Too many young ones die premature deaths due to preventable diseases. Countless others have been abducted to fight as child soldiers or to serve as forced laborers or domestic slaves. Those who escape these tragic fates often find themselves orphaned by ebola or the AIDS pandemic. They are confined to refugee camps where neglect, disease, and hunger are the only certainties. Father Dunson met these children. He went to the places they call home, he listened to their painful and courageous stories. Now he tells their stories to the world, so that he may enlist the world's help for them.

Yet the vision that inspired this book extends far beyond Uganda. It is the vision of human solidarity, and its scope is worldwide. This vision calls attention to the deplorable conditions of children in all parts of the world, not only in Africa but also in Asia, Europe, and the Americas, both North and South. The book documents real cases of real children, to show that the evils of hunger, sexual exploitation, and physical and emotional cruelty are without boundaries. It illustrates the life-long impact on the world's youth of inadequate health care and the lack of educational opportunity. It tells the tragic stories of missing, abandoned, and abducted children who grow up without family, without friends, without play, and frequently without hope. It paints a portrait of human suffering, captured on the face of a child.

Throughout the book, however, images of tragic destruction and abuse are countered by striking symbols of heroic action. The "missing" children brutally abducted in Buenos Aires are loved and remembered by their grandmothers. These courageous women meet weekly in the Plaza de Mayo to walk silently, carrying enlarged photos of the children, so that the world will not forget them. Young people degraded by pornography spread across the Internet may someday hear of the tireless work of Father Fortunato Di Noto, the Sicilian priest who used his outrage over their degradation to become an indispensable help to international detectives who eventually broke up a global pedophile ring. The hungry children of Asia and Africa may soon benefit from Professor Amartya Sen's Nobel Prize–winning lifework. He has dedicated himself to making known the political and social causes of starvation and malnutrition.

So, besides alarming us, these pages help us to believe that the damage done to the world's children is not irreparable. There are persons and groups willing to help, willing to risk their lives and share their resources so that the lives of endangered children may be saved. Father Dunson points to a wide variety of individuals and organizations struggling to alleviate the suffering of children. He traces the pastoral zeal of the Catholic Church, inspired by the writings and example of Pope John Paul II, whose fidelity to World Youth Day has brought hope to millions. He shows the consistent efforts of the United Nations, which through its humanitarian agencies invited five hundred children to be delegates to its General Assembly to speak for their brothers and sisters worldwide. He recalls the altruistic work of groups like Human Rights Watch, World Vision, the International Medical Corps, and many others whose hands-on services are often the first and sometimes the only caring human touch these children feel. His stories take us to tiny but powerful places of outreach like Casa Alianza in Guatemala City, a Central American branch of Covenant House, and Casa Madre, where Ursuline Sisters minister to HIV/AIDS children in Youngstown, Ohio. These and other poignant examples of tender, generous care for children serve as signs of hope for otherwise hopeless youth and encourage us to strive for a human solidarity that will protect them.

In this passionate book, Father Dunson speaks for the most vulnerable children of God. His is an urgent call for human solidarity issued both locally and globally. It is a reminder that the anger and outrage we feel must be countered with love, a love born of knowledge and awareness, the love that Jesus taught. As a moral theologian, Father Dunson knows that God's love needs to be put into action. As a seminary professor, he is aware that unless people learn about needs, they cannot respond to them. As a child advocate, he brings the world's invisible youth out into the light. As an author, he touches our hearts and mobilizes our spirits. We cannot fail to respond.

As you enter into the stories told in this book, I pray that the Lord may stir your heart to compassionate action that will transform the suffering of the world's children into redemptive love.

Archbishop John Baptist Odama
Gulu, Uganda

Acknowledgments

I have been fortunate in writing this book. From the very beginning, many of my friends offered enthusiastic encouragement. The faculty, staff, and administration of St. Mary Seminary and Graduate School of Theology in Cleveland encouraged me to undertake the project and granted me an academic sabbatical in order to conduct research in East Central Africa. My longtime friends Peter and Diana Opio of Kampala, Uganda, opened their home to me in 2001, offering unfailing personal support. Their three daughters, Jessie, Josephine (my goddaughter), and Rose brightened my memorable stay in Africa with their laughter, their play, and their spontaneous embrace of life.

Numerous colleagues and friends read preliminary drafts and offered judicious insights that contributed substantively to the final text. My Ursuline friends Rosemarie Carfagna, Donna Marie Bradesca, and Mary McCormick, as well as Father Paul Hritz and my nephew James A. Dunson III—all generously gave of their time and talent in this enterprise. Alan Rome, librarian at St. Mary Seminary, offered invaluable research assistance throughout the project. Secretarial support from Lori Eppich, Terri Zakraysek, and Bertha Popovic was of great assistance in the final preparation of the manuscript. I have been blessed in having Susan Perry as my editor at Orbis Books. Virtually every page of this book has benefited from her expertise and acumen.

I happily dedicate this work to my parents, Ann and Jim Dunson, who nurtured six sons into adulthood. I will be eternally grateful that I was gifted by God with their love.

David Snyder, Catholic Relief Services. Used with permission.

Young girl awaiting off-loading of a humanitarian barge
in Bena Dibele, Congo, March 2001.

Introduction:
A Child's Face

E very human face is an epiphany. In the face of the other, especially the vulnerable other, is a wordless call that awakens us to solidarity, to our connection with that other.

On August 2, 1999, a mechanic at Zaventem airport in Brussels saw two faces that will remain forever etched in his memory. While he was undertaking a routine examination of the landing gear of an Airbus run by Sabena Belgian World Airlines, he suddenly found himself gazing at the frozen faces of two African boys, teenage stowaways from Guinea who had hoped to enter Europe.

Fodé Tounkara, age fifteen, and Yaguine Koita, age fourteen, had hidden in that landing gear. They had died of exposure on their way to a future they had hoped would be a liberation out of the despair of poverty. In fact, their bodies had likely made several round trips from Africa to Europe before being found.

The boys must have known that such a journey held deadly perils, because they had written a message that would speak for them if they didn't survive. This heartrending note, found stuffed in one of their pockets, acknowledged frankly the terrible cost they were willing to pay. Their message was, in essence: If you see that we have sacrificed ourselves and lost our lives, it is because we suffer too much.

Fodé and Yaguine had set off for Europe not for themselves alone, but as representatives of a whole generation of young Africans seeking solidarity with the people of the Northern Hemisphere. They traveled with the expectation that they might appeal to the hearts of Europeans to see in them brothers in the one human family. Fodé and Yaguine wanted opportunities to learn, to be free from the persistent burden of hunger, and to live in a society that was not torn apart by violence. In other words, they went in desperate search of what we all desire for our own children.

They were two idealistic boys, bursting with energy like most adolescents. Perhaps, naively, they just wanted to be comforted in the assurance that they were not alone in their search for a better world. I have often reflected upon that carefully prepared note that has become their voice. It poignantly reveals the aspirations of the youngest—and therefore the most vulnerable—generation in the human family. Their words remind us that young people across the globe continue to be the first to see and embrace the ties that bind us to each other. I suspect that a teacher or an adult mentor helped them to craft this letter, to aid them in giving expression to their deep longings for a world different from the one they knew. In their note, Fodé and Yaguine addressed the leaders of Europe:

> We have the honor and pleasure of addressing this letter to you, with the greatest confidence, to explain why we are making this voyage and to tell you of the suffering of the children and young people in Africa. But first of all we would like to send you the most innocent, sweet and respectful greetings possible. We appeal to you, for the love of your beautiful continent and in the name of our Creator, God Almighty, who has given you the experience, wealth and power to build and organize your continent so that it can become the most beautiful and most greatly admired friend of others. We appeal to your solidarity and kindness to help the people of Africa. Please help us, for we in Africa are suffering enormously; please help us, for we have many problems and not enough children's rights.
>
> By way of problems, we have war, disease, and famine. As regards children's rights, we have schools in Africa, especially in Guinea, but very little teaching, except in private schools, where you can get a good education—but for this

you need a large sum of money and our parents are poor. So, you see, we are prepared to make sacrifices, and even risk our lives, because there is too much suffering in Africa and we need you to help us combat poverty and to make sure there is no more war in Africa. That said, we would like to study and we ask you to help us to study so that there are people like you in Africa. And, last but not least, we beseech you to excuse us for daring to write this letter to such important people, for whom we have the greatest respect. And please do not forget that only you can help Africa to overcome its weakness.

No wonder Fodé and Yaguine were willing to risk everything on a seemingly foolish and deadly trip to Europe. They sensed acutely the gravity of the situation in their homeland, as well as their own vulnerability, and sought to make others aware of that truth. They died attempting to communicate to us how precarious life had become for many on their continent. They did not survive, but their message did.

Louis Michel, the vice prime minister of Belgium, distributed this letter to each of his colleagues, the leaders of Europe, vowing: "We cannot leave this cry without a response. We must return hope to Africa." I doubt that Fodé and Yaguine wanted the Europeans to solve all their problems or mold them into Europeans. Rather, they were simply attempting to live out their hope of gaining greater control over their own destiny. They had been led to believe that they would meet many people in Europe who shared their own intense desire to eradicate suffering. They knew that Christians in distant lands held to the same moral conviction that they had, namely, that every child of earth is a child of God. Their parents and catechists had taught them that they possessed an inherent dignity that originates in being created in the very image of God. They wanted to befriend these people in faraway lands who might see God in them and who possessed the means to help bring them to a better day. At the same time, they knew themselves to be terribly vulnerable.

All the children of earth are vulnerable. By the Creator's providential design, each of us must begin life's journey utterly helpless. We cannot secure life for ourselves. Only if others embrace us with their gifts of nurture can we survive our childhood. The human species after birth has the longest dependency period of any of earth's creatures. From the very first moment that the hands of another human being lift us from the womb, we must rely on others to feed us, protect us, teach us, and love us into life. This is our fate. This is what it means to be human. From birth to death, no one is ever truly independent. All of us need each other, more at some times than at others. Our mutual need is both human and holy.

There is a covenant we human beings hold with our youngest members and it is their sole guarantee of life. Kofi Annan, the Secretary General of the United Nations, recently spoke of that covenant, saying: "There is no trust more sacred than the one the world holds with children. There is no duty more important than ensuring that their rights are respected, that their welfare is protected, that their lives are free from fear and want, and that they grow up in peace." From his position of power, Annan was calling the world's attention to those who are powerless.

As the human family enters the third millennium, approximately eleven million of our children under five years of age continue to die each year from malnutrition or preventable diseases— that is, from a lack of love, solidarity, and human resourcefulness dedicated to them and their well-being.[1] Because they are, de facto, the weakest link in the human chain, their fate is entirely dependent on solidarity with the stronger members. That solidarity is tenuous in our world today. The suffering of children in our cities as well as in the poorest countryside is an open wound, a festering sore that calls into question our very humanity: Do we possess hearts that know how to nurture our own offspring?

The nurture that is the right of every child is most needed where it is most difficult to guarantee: in those areas of the world where the seemingly intractable grip of violence, poverty, and devastating epidemics subjects our children daily to fear and desolation. The sad and distant look in their eyes presents us with an unavoidable mandate to act on their behalf. Their eyes call out, "Protect me. Care for me. Make it possible for me to live."

Our young and impressionable daughters and sons are at risk not only from these physical threats but also from harmful cultural forces. Wherever male children are accorded favoritism in terms of respect and access to opportunities and resources denied to their female counterparts, something is terribly wrong in the human family. We jeopardize not only the safety and well-being of our young girls but also our own identity as a moral and just people. Wherever economic practices reduce young people to commodities or persuade them to believe that only those who can make it on their own are worthy of respect, then our promise to teach them the truth has been broken. Whenever any child is erroneously led to believe that love and affection can be earned, then we have barred that child from life's simplest and deepest joy.

Where does the moral call to solidarity originate? The French philosopher Emmanuel Levinas holds that it is not from my innermost self, but rather from the other that the call to morality emanates. My own moral sense leads me to believe that Levinas is right. He has developed penetrating insights into the radical unity that exists within our one human family. We are linked to every other person by bonds that are both visible and invisible. Levinas holds that we are inexplicably drawn close to the invisible bond whenever we gaze into the face of the other. When we open ourselves to discovering the true face of the other, we also encounter our own identity. In other words, our identity is in some mysterious, inexplicable way bound up with that of our fellow human companions, with their lives and their destiny. Therefore we are most self-possessed when we see and respond to the ethical appeal coming from the face of the other.

The frozen faces of Fodé and Yaguine first moved the airline mechanic who discovered them and then their silent message reached across Europe and beyond, piercing the hearts of many. At certain intimate moments, the face of a beloved calls for joy in the experience of loving surrender. At other times, the look of pain on the face of a stranger can hold out a plea for compassion that is impossible to ignore.

Speaking of the moment of disclosure that happens whenever we look upon the face of the other, Levinas tells us:

> There is first the very uprightness of the face, its upright exposure, without defence. The skin of the face is that which stays most naked, most destitute. It is the most naked, though with a decent nudity. It is the most destitute also: there is an essential poverty in the face, the proof of this is that one tries to mask this poverty by putting on poses, by taking on a countenance. The face is exposed, menaced, as if inviting us to an act of violence. At the same time, the face is what forbids us to kill.[2]

At another time in history, Nazi soldiers were absolutely forbidden to look into the eyes of those detained and murdered in their concentration camps. Why? Perhaps because in the eyes of a victim they might see a fellow human being, alive just like themselves, but in grave jeopardy. That is why the tormentor had to seek to deprive the victim of his humanity. Otherwise, the ethical appeal in the face of the vulnerable other might be impossible to resist. This is precisely why such a plea had to be crushed at its inception—at the moment of connection, of looking upon the face of the other.

The human story is replete with examples of our endless attempts to speak—and, at desperate moments, to shout or scream—the truth about ourselves to our companions, oftentimes without ever uttering a word. It has been like this from the beginning. Eons ago, we drew pictures on the walls of our caves to communicate with others. Through gazing into the eyes of the other we connect with each other in the most personal way possible. Haven't we all noticed how the eyes of children, especially those too young to speak, are so revealing? Indeed, the face of every child possesses an extraordinary, grace-filled capacity to move us beyond ourselves. It should not be surprising, then, that some of the most memorable photographs of the twentieth century have been photos of children. There are abundant examples of the faces of children stirring us to an intimate sympathy with young ones who suffer on account of the cruelty of their elders.

The social conscience of the American people was shaken to the core by Huynh Cong Ut's 1972 Pulitzer prize–winning photo of a terrified Vietnamese girl who just had the clothes napalmed off her. Millions of people sensed in an acute way the pain of so many young lives being destroyed. Suddenly, the unfolding tragedy in Southeast Asia had a human face, the face of a little girl.

In 1993, while visiting famine-stricken Sudan, the South African photojournalist Kevin Carter took a photograph that made the world weep. Carter was in the village of Ayod, snapping photos of famine victims and becoming increasingly depressed. Seeking relief from the sight of masses of people starving to death, he wandered into the open bush searching for a quiet moment alone. The stillness was broken by a soft, high-pitched whimpering. He discovered, lying in the dust, a severely malnourished girl who was struggling to crawl to a feeding station. As she collapsed in the dirt, a waiting vulture made his approach. This child's image has become an icon of African anguish.

The grandmothers of the Plaza de Mayo in the center of Buenos Aires, Argentina, still gather faithfully once a week to keep alive the memory and the spirit of their missing children. They hold up large posters emblazoned with the faces of their missing young ones. Everyone who passes by encounters these images. Tens of millions of people around the world see them in newspapers and on television. These faces trouble the heart and challenge the curious mind to question the circumstances that surrounded their disappearance.

The ethical appeal in the face of a child is not reserved only to the starving, missing, or wounded children in our midst. No, it is universal. We can see it everywhere, but perhaps most especially in the faces of our own children. The first moment in which a mother or father gazes upon the face of a newborn child is a holy moment filled with promise. Canadian theologian Ronald Rolheiser captures well the ethical appeal that emanates from the sight of our own offspring. He writes: "Perhaps there is nothing in this world as powerful to break selfishness as is the simple act of looking at our own children. In our love for them we are given a privileged avenue to feel as God feels—to burst in unselfishness, in joy, in delight, and in the desire to let another's life be more real and important than our own."[3]

It was while I was still a teenager that I was first powerfully drawn to the writings of the French theologian Pierre Teilhard de Chardin. This poet-priest once defined the human person as evolution become conscious of itself. In other words, the human person is the creature who knows and "who knows that he knows." Chardin predicted that the day would come when, after mastering the physical universe, we would look to harness for God the energies of love. We are destined to become ever more conscious of the interdependence of all creation and to be drawn into a deepening kinship with the most vulnerable in our midst. Perhaps the very frailty of our youngest and weakest members will, at long last, be perceived as humanity's great treasure, our teacher in the inscrutable ways of God. After all, when humanity and divinity met, it was in the person of a helpless, utterly dependent, completely vulnerable child named Jesus.

In the human family there have always been those who have perceived frailty and vulnerability solely as burden. Yet, for the believing Christian, the face of the vulnerable other can never be simply the source of an unavoidable moral demand that we otherwise might wish to shun. No, in the first instance, the other comes to us as gift of God, a treasure bearing a mysterious likeness to the Creator. Our God has an overwhelming, divine desire to be enfleshed now in the ongoing human drama. The awesome mystery of the incarnation unfolds for us in our day every time we see the Christ Child in every child who walks the earth. I believe that God lies hidden and helpless in the children everywhere who just want a chance to experience the joy of being loved into life.

God breathes in Sunday Obote, a fifteen-year-old boy whom I met in northern Uganda and who had been kidnapped and thrown into war for eight years in southern Sudan. We can meet God in the young street children of Mexico City, children who, just like Jesus, have nowhere to call home. God's body can be reverenced in Siri, a young Thai girl who was sold against her will when she was only fifteen years old to a brothel in Ubon Ratchitani in northeastern Thailand. These children have suffered the loss of their parents, the loss of their innocence, and the loss of their childhoods. They have been scorned by many, yet to the discerning eye—the eye of faith—God lies hidden in them. God waits in them for the power of goodness to overcome the evils that have been inflicted upon the human family's most vulnerable ones.

Thomas Merton, in his masterpiece *Raids on the Unspeakable*, offers us a clue as to why God would choose to be present in secret in humanity's wounded children. Merton writes:

> Into this world, this demented inn, in which there is absolutely no room for Him at all, Christ has come uninvited. But because He cannot be at home in it, because He is out of place in it, and yet he must be in it, His place is with those others for whom there is no room. His place is with those who do not belong, who are rejected by power because they are regarded as weak, those who are discredited, who are denied the status of persons, who are tortured, bombed and exterminated. With those for whom there is no room, Christ is present in the world. He is mysteriously present in those for whom there seems to be nothing but the world at its worst.[4]

All across our world, children are falling victim to powerful forces beyond their control, forces that sabotage the bright promise tomorrow should bear for them. Never before has the world faced the possibility of so many orphans. The expectation of secure love and hope in the future that is so natural to young children is being replaced by the reality of rejection and near despair when death from the AIDS pandemic robs millions of children of their parents. Civil strife, profit-driven conflicts, and ethnic battles have forced countless numbers of families to seek safe haven outside their own countries, to live as modern-day nomads far from their homes, painfully separated from the people they love. Parents are exhausted from their daily fight for survival as they see the bright future they had hoped for their children fade more and more each day.

There are more children alive now than there have been at any other moment in human history. Two billion children crave nothing more than a chance at a peaceful, more just world than exists today. Indeed, over one-third of the entire world population is under fifteen years old. In our day, 95 percent of world population growth is taking place in the developing countries of the world. Many of these nations are currently being robbed of their future vitality by the multiple afflictions that have been unleashed on children. Adding to these afflictions is the massive indifference of most of the world to the plight of vulnerable children. Today's human family is young and its future is in danger.

What is certain is that the God Christians worship, a God of triune love, stands with these young ones. If you want to draw close to the creative presence of God, simply wrap your arms around the body of a small child yearning to grow. The Redeemer's heart burns with desire in the bodies of doctors and researchers struggling for a new world set free from malaria, hunger, AIDS, measles, polio, tuberculosis, diphtheria, whooping cough, and all the preventable infectious diseases that harm and kill life at its beginning. The Holy Spirit is the comforter and companion of all those children who walk the earth alone and who just yearn to be touched with the hand of love. There is no indifference in God—God has made an irrevocable decision as to where He will dwell—yet many of us fail to notice.

In our day we are, at long last, awakening to the wisdom of our youngest. Some eighty heads of state gathered in New York City in May 2002 for a landmark UN General Assembly at which more than five hundred children served as delegates. Never before had the voices of children been welcomed to the deliberations of humanity's most powerful leaders. It will be years before the impact of those voices will be felt. But they, like Fodé and Yaguine, have the capacity to speak to the heart of the world.

The nineteenth-century charismatic preacher Henry Ward Beecher once observed that children are the hands by which we take hold of heaven. If this is true, it is also likely that in the movement toward a more peaceful and harmonious earth it will be the children who lead the way. At festivities marking World Youth Day in Toronto, Canada, in the summer of 2002 Pope John Paul II testified to this when he said: "Too many lives begin and end without joy, without hope. Young people are coming together to commit themselves, in the strength of their faith in Jesus Christ, to the great cause of peace and human solidarity."

In the faces of our children we are given the best glimpse of humanity's future, a preview of the world to come. This is why there can be no moral issue more unifying, more urgent, or more universal than nurturing their well-being and securing their chance to embrace the life our Creator destined for them.

Notes

1. See *The State of The World's Children: 2003*. This report is published yearly by the United Nations agency UNICEF and documents critical statistics such as child mortality rates, literacy rates, and life expectancy rates in individual nations as well as in regions of the world. It can be accessed at the website: www.unicef.org.

2. Emmanuel Levinas, *Ethics and Infinity* (Pittsburgh, Penn.: Duquesne University Press, 1985), 86.

3. Ronald Rolheiser, *The Holy Longing: The Search for a Christian Spirituality* (New York: Doubleday, 1999), 192.

4. Thomas Merton, *Raids on the Unspeakable* (New York: New Directions, 1964), 72–73.

Clarence Williams, The Photo Project/Burundi. Used with permission.

Ntirandekura, 16, under pressure to register for the army
in Burundi, poses with his hand-made gun.

1
Growing Up with the Rebels

Spend one afternoon at Gusco Camp and I promise you it will be impossible ever again to take for granted the joys of your childhood.

Gusco (Gulu United to Save the Children Organization) is a non-governmental organization that runs a camp in northern Uganda for several hundred formerly abducted children. On the afternoon of July 4, 2001, while I was a guest at this site, I encountered a band of children bonded together by a terrible fate—each one had been kidnapped by rebels in the Lord's Resistance Army (LRA) and thrown into war.

The LRA is one of the world's most treacherous guerrilla forces. It is currently operating in the southern Sudan and refreshing its numbers by kidnapping children and adolescents to serve as its soldiers. The leader of this ill-defined rebel band, Joseph Kony, is unable to attract enough adult followers willing to fight alongside him, so he fills the ranks with abducted children. Nearly 60 percent of this insurgency movement is made up of children under the age of sixteen. The children I met at Gusco were escapees from the LRA. They would remain in the camp for some six to eight weeks, preparing to be reintegrated into their families and communities.

These so-called child soldiers had been robbed of their childhood, held as captives by the LRA rebels, and forced into living nightmares. After having being abducted, each of them was made to trek long distances between northern Uganda and southern Sudan laden down with stolen food, goods, and arms. If they cried, they were beaten. If they cried again, they were shot or their necks were broken with an iron bar. The female children were used as sex slaves, trophies given to the top officers in the LRA as rewards for military victories. Within the first three months of captivity, every boy was trained in the use of weapons and told that his gun was now "his mother, his best friend, his everything." These children were routinely used as human shields to protect the adults who were abusing and committing atrocities against them.

On that memorable afternoon I found myself listening to a nearly unbelievable story related to me by Sunday Obote, a fifteen-year-old boy. There was a genuineness in his facial expressions and tone of voice that made me like him immediately. Speaking with calm self-confidence, Sunday explained that he had been abducted when he was just seven years old. In fact, he told me, he wasn't actually sure how old he had been when the LRA kidnapped him during a night raid on his home. He later asked his captors how old he was and they told him he was seven, so he believed them. In the early weeks of his captivity he never once cried; he was too frightened by what he saw inflicted on those who did. Instead, he kept in his mind an image of the faces of his mother and father. This alone comforted him and gave him the strength to continue to live.

Death was no stranger to Sunday; he had experienced it daily. On orders from the rebels in the LRA he had killed other children and many adults. This child, who sat serenely with me in the shade, who smiled at me whenever I smiled at him, had lost his freedom, his entire childhood, and certainly a vital part of his humanity in the hellish company of Joseph Kony. After military skirmishes he was often instructed to eat his next meal seated on dead enemy bodies. This young, impressionable boy was told that through this action he would be gifted with whatever courage the enemy possessed. He believed the rebels' words. What alternative did he have?

As weeks became months and months became years, those who had kidnapped him became his family. They were his only human contact. He grew emotionally hardened in carrying out the savage orders of the LRA officers, in responding to the shout so often heard: "Kill—or be killed!"

Sunday eventually became part of the elite corps of bodyguards that surrounds the notorious and feared Joseph Kony. His special assignment was to go on expeditions to secure new girls for Kony's pleasure. Sunday confided to me: "When I was about twelve years old, they began to trust me to help abduct women for Kony, to abduct beautiful girls only for Kony. The soldiers who were given women were always the top leaders. Once I made the mistake of bringing them an ugly girl. I was beaten."

When I met Sunday, he was in the seventh week of his freedom, having been rescued by Ugandan security forces in a surprise ambush on the LRA in May 2001. Sunday has a bullet lodged in his leg, a souvenir of his eight-year captivity in the bush of southern Sudan. Regrettably, the emotional wounds he bears are far more serious. The staff at Gusco told me that the war trauma he has suffered will necessitate his being at the camp for a long time. His self-confident demeanor hides a most vulnerable adolescent.

Sunday is one of many unfortunate children being cared for at Gusco. Among the common side-effects that afflict formerly abducted children who have been brutalized in war are eating disorders, aggressive and militaristic behavior, epileptic fits, alcohol abuse, and the inability to form trusting relationships. Their terrorizing ordeals come back to them in flashbacks and nightmares. Many of the girls who escape bear the scourge of the sexually transmitted diseases with which they have been infected.

Children at Gusco Camp can remember long periods of time when they had little or nothing to eat while living with the rebels. On some days all that was available to them as food were leaves that had fallen to the ground or bark from the trees. Now that food is available to them, those prolonged periods of food deprivation continue to wreak havoc. Many of the children fall victim to eating either too little or too much food.

The pain of their ordeal is well understood by the staff at Gusco Camp. These skilled and compassionate adults have a single mission: to help the children reclaim their lives from their captors and ultimately be free of the fears that dominated their lives while in captivity. At Gusco there is food and medicine. There are educational opportunities and, most important, there is a chance to forge a whole new life. Yet the long journey from shattered innocence to restored hope begins only when these young ones can again believe that the adult world that surrounds them will not harm them. Our collective failure to protect these children has deeply wounded their trust in the adult world.

It appears that Sunday's personal struggles center on his inability to form trusting relationships. He has twice experienced a radical sense of abandonment. As a child he lost his family when he was kidnapped by the rebels. Now, as a teenager, he is experiencing separation from the rebels in whose company he grew up. He tells me that his greatest hope is that his rebel brothers come out of the conflict alive. In the meantime, he wonders about whom he can trust and where he really belongs.

The rebels are experts in destroying bonds of trust and of love, especially the parental bond. Their objective is to get the children to believe that they belong to the rebel group, and the rebel group alone. In some extreme cases, rebel leaders have resorted to physically coercing the children into killing their own parents. This is the final blow to any connectedness to their past for these children. There will be no hidden dreams of reunion with family; there is no one to return to if they dare to attempt escaping. The children are victims of the ultimate manipulation: they have been forced to kill the very people who care about them the most.

The day I visited Gusco, which was American Independence Day, the 2,867th young person to graduate from the camp walked out the front gate into a free but uncertain future. At the age of twelve, he is now fully retired from the military.

Every day is freedom day at Gusco. Every child here is destined to be reunited with loved ones back home. Parents feel exhilaration in the simple yet astounding fact that a son or daughter is still alive, since many abducted children in this region of war-weary Africa never return. During the last decade only half of the abducted children in northern Uganda have managed to escape and return home.

The anxiety of some parents is nearly overwhelming. They know all too well what it feels like to be helpless to protect their own offspring from a violent world. One father of two sons who had been kidnapped tried to give me his sons; he begged me to take them home with me, so terrified was he of their being re-abducted. Some parents fear that their children will never fit into society after having survived warfare but will remain scarred by the trauma and brutality that characterized their daily lives, in some cases for many years. Some of the children become desensitized to suffering as a result of their prolonged exposure to overwhelming violence. Parents are sometimes fearful of taking their own children back, because the rebels' dehumanizing tactics have toughened them and made them extremely hostile.

When I walked on the grounds of the camp I could sense that this was a place of promise that held out the hope of new beginnings. I witnessed the healing and liberating spirit that flourishes there. I saw young people learning music and dance, while other children were busy cooking the supper that would soon be shared in common. Now it appears to me that they were befriending each other, instead of their guns.

Meanwhile, armed guards posted at every entrance to this site protect the children around the clock. It is widely known that the LRA is set upon recapturing these escapees. The sight of the guards, as well as the anguish of that father pleading with me to take custody of his sons, let me know just how fragile is the new freedom these children now experience.

As my conversation with Sunday drew to a close, he asked what seems to me an astounding question. With near glee he inquired: "Do you know that there are people here who love me?" This teenager, who had lost so much of his life to an evil that few of us can even begin to imagine, obviously had not forgotten what love is like. This, I suspect, will prove to be his redemption.

A LOST IDENTITY

I was struck with the realization that Sunday had systematically and methodically been made to banish from consciousness all that lingered of his former self—all of childhood's tenderness in the secure company of parents who loved him. From the moment he was abducted from his home, he never heard his name pronounced again. Never. It was as if he had never been given a name. It would be eight long years until he would know the bliss of hearing the sound of his mother's voice, and when he did, she was joyfully shouting his name! What he heard was something that many abducted children never hear.

The uniqueness of human life is celebrated every time parents designate a name for their new child. To be given a name is, in some real way, also to be gifted with an awareness of your own special identity in the family. Those who know and love you recognize you in a distinctive way that is reserved for you—by calling you by name. In the strategy of depersonalization undertaken by the Nazi regime during the Second World War, those detained in concentration camps were similarly denied the opportunity to be called by name. They were given numbers instead, numbers burned into their arms, and these numbers served as identification. They were treated like objects, not persons, which is precisely the lot of child soldiers today.

Children thrust into guerrilla warfare lose not only their innocence but also their identity and individuality. They come to be known only by a generic title such as "the boys" or *kadogo,* a Swahili term meaning "tough little one." This change of name signifies the complete depersonalization of the child. Some children have been called "Suicide," "Rambo," and "Strike Commando"—names that are symbols of death.

The identity of an individual human being makes sense only in the context of relationships with others. For instance, I can identify myself as a brother, friend, uncle, and so on, and actively participate in those relationships. How devastating it must be to a person's sense of identity to be suddenly plucked out of these vital relationships and forced into a radically different context. How tragic it is when this happens to a young child who is especially in need of loving relationships to foster self-identity. Young people forced into warfare soon discover that those who control them have one driving desire—to maximize their labor while minimizing their individuality. The child soldier is seen as merely an object ripe for exploitation. It is not that uncommon for these children to be bought and sold like objects, their very personhood denied.

In March, 1999, some children who had been kidnapped by the LRA ended up being sold to the terrorist Osama bin Laden. He purchased them as cheap laborers to work in his marijuana fields in Sudan. Abducted children were selected at the LRA's headquarters in Jubelin. They were then moved to Nsitu camp, where Arab slave dealers purchased some of them. These children were transported to Juba airport and flown to bin Laden's camps in the Nile Valley, north of Khartoum. Just as Jacob's son Joseph was sold into slavery by his brothers in Old Testament times, children in our day are still being handed over to those who traffic in the buying and selling of persons.

I conducted interviews with fifteen former child soldiers in the Great Lakes region of Africa in July 2001. They ranged in age from eight to seventeen. All of them had been kidnapped from their families. They had all either escaped from their rebel captors or been rescued by government forces. The shortest period of captivity for these children was three months; the longest was eight years. Twelve of the fifteen had been forced to kill. As they told me their stories, it became clear to me that the rebels had preyed on the children's instinct for self-preservation. Every effort had been made to persuade the new child soldiers into believing that their only chance at staying alive was based on their carrying out the unspeakably brutal orders of their captors.

Likewise, in very calculated ways, the rebels attempted to destroy the children's personalities. This required deadening—or at least dulling—any deeply personal feelings, especially the distinctively human response that stirs compassion when encountering someone in peril. True stories of children in peril hover over Africa.

ABDUCTED GIRLS

On the night of October 9, 1996, 139 girls between twelve and fifteen years old were abducted from St. Mary's, a Catholic boarding school in Aboke, Uganda. The next day their headmistress, Sister Rachele, went in pursuit of the rebels to beg for the return of her girls. Surprisingly, the LRA were won over by this very persuasive Italian nun, but she managed to secure the freedom of only 109 of them. Joseph Kony had sent orders to his commanders to be sure to keep thirty of the girls. He would use them as personal gifts to his friends and top military officers while keeping three for himself. As of today, nineteen of these girls remain in captivity. Pope John Paul II at the Vatican and Kofi Annan at the United Nations have made futile appeals for their release. Stories of the ordeals these children have been forced to endure live in the collective consciousness of the Ugandan people. Professor Els De Temmerman, a Belgian journalist and child rights advocate, has chronicled the horrific events that surround their captivity in a powerful new book entitled *Aboke Girls: Children Abducted in Northern Uganda.*[1]

Among the unfortunate thirty who were chosen at random to remain behind with the rebels was Agnes Gillian Ocitti, then a fourteen-year-old known among her classmates as the most resourceful in the group. Sister Rachele told Agnes and the others who were to remain with the rebels not to look at the girls being freed as they began their departure for home. Agnes realized that Sister Rachele feared that the girls who were staying might cry at this sight and would be beaten for their tears. The loss of a loving farewell was just the beginning of Agnes's pain.

Agnes can vividly recall the first horror she experienced in the company of the soldiers. During their first week in the bush one desperately frightened child, a twelve-year-old girl, had hidden in a small hut in an attempt to escape. The rebels shouted to Agnes and the other new recruits: "Find her! If you don't find her, we will kill one of you instead." The child was found. Rebels pounced on her immediately, and one of them stomped repeatedly on her chest. The dark scene that unfolded saw not only the cruel death of a young child but also a cold and deliberate attempt to destroy the humanity of the others.

After the soldiers had taken turns beating the child mercilessly, Agnes and the other girls, all new to the raw savagery of the LRA, were given the command to "finish her off." Agnes's entire body trembled in disbelief. She knew herself and realized she just couldn't do this. It was the first command she had been given by her captors that would have to go unanswered. What Agnes couldn't have been expected to know was that her captors were skilled in crushing humane instincts like the ones welling up inside her at that moment. Agnes's feelings of compassion intensified as she saw in the beaten girl's eyes a silent plea for help.

The rebels were bent on destroying what Agnes knew about herself. The children were ordered to collect sticks of firewood that would serve a double purpose, as weapons to strike the girl and as fuel to cook the next meal. Upon direct orders to strike the already bleeding child, the children formed a circle around the girl and began to hit her lightly, directing all their blows to her legs. The soldiers stopped them. They took over, insisting on showing the new recruits the proper method. What was called for, they demonstrated, were swift blows to either the neck or the back of the head. The children were all crying at this point as they were made to line up and individually follow the example set by the rebels. Those who did not strike hard enough were punished and made to repeat their blows to the victim.

Agnes was frantically trying to plot some possible escape from this ordeal. It is common among new, abducted child soldiers to invent mechanisms to hide their true selves, their innocence and their refusal to kill. She began to imagine that she was not inside her body. She pretended to leave her body, momentarily, in order to do the unthinkable. When it was her turn to strike, Agnes joined in the deadly assault.

When the girl no longer responded to the force of the blows, Agnes had an overwhelming sense that this single action had separated her from her past in an irrevocable way. Life just couldn't ever be the same for her again. She believed she was now and forever cut off from the good person she once had been back home in the sanctuary of her family's love.

Through this savage event and other equally brutal actions it was impressed upon Agnes and the other newly abducted children that unswerving allegiance to the group was absolutely demanded. Conformity to the will of the rebel leaders was now to be stressed above every personal emotion. Empathetic feelings, in particular, had to be crushed and never expressed.

New recruits are initiated through a ritual ceremony in which their bodies are anointed with oil on their heads, chest, and back. The oil is to strengthen them for the coming battles and to bind them to each other through a shared rite of entrance into the group. In this ceremony they symbolically leave behind their former selves and take on a new, corporate identity as part of the rebel force. The indoctrination of child soldiers under Joseph Kony's rule includes being told that the anointing has miraculous powers to stop the bullets of the enemy from harming them.

The monstrous pressure tactics that the rebels use to get conformity from their new recruits destroy a lifetime of emotional normalcy with alarming quickness. However, Agnes never fully acquiesced to her ruthless captors. She cleverly pretended to be manipulated by them in order to lull them into believing she belonged to them. The rebels were able to force conformity and even break down her identity, but they were unable to obtain her authentic allegiance. When she learned that Kony had promised her to a commander older than her father, she resolved to escape or die attempting it. The very morning of her escape, she managed to save the life of an old man whom the rebels would certainly have killed had Agnes not kept silent about his whereabouts.

When a government helicopter suddenly appeared overhead at around 9:00 in the morning, surprising her brigade, she felt it was God's providence. In that graced moment she was seized by a new sense of courage. She grabbed the hand of a classmate named Esther and together they fled in the confusion. They hid in the high grass, motionless, for a very long time. Afterward they ran so fast and so far that the rebels didn't have a chance to catch them. That night, safe in an army barracks in Palenga, Agnes and Esther cried with joy and then fell into a deep, peaceful sleep, side by side.

The staff at Gusco Camp informed me that there is a ritual for their new residents, those fortunate enough to have escaped the clutches of the rebels. To celebrate the freedom and new life of these children, the clothes they were wearing while in the company of the rebels are burned in their presence, and new clothes are given to them. These new clothes are a gift from the community to which they are returning. The gift is meant to reinforce in the minds and hearts of the recipients that they are indeed welcomed back and that the violence they were forced to perform will not be held against them. Yet it would take a monumental act of grace for these abused sons and daughters to return home with the conviction that their dreaded past had actually been forgiven. They know from having listened to the radio while in captivity that everyone in East Central Africa has heard of the killings that happened in the fields and all the inhuman actions they were forced to perform simply in order to survive. Still, most of the children feel that some of their shame is lifted when the fire burns a piece of their past. It is a first step on their long road to healing.

Sunday emerged from captivity with the LRA rebels with a bullet in his leg and deep emotional wounds. Agnes escaped with one overriding question haunting her: "Will I ever be the same again?" Against all odds, these young people can still sense some hopefulness about their future. Best of all, today they live in the company of people who love and value them. What was once lost is now slowly being restored. As I spoke with Sunday he remained incredulous that there were people in this world who could love him. Over time, Agnes has gradually come to believe more in her own core goodness again. Her character, her personality, and her solidarity with others in jeopardy were not destroyed by the soldiers. They never fully possessed her. It takes a very special kind of courage to face inhuman circumstances, as Agnes did, and not allow oneself to be consumed by them.

Child soldiers like Sunday and Agnes are made to endure the world at its worst: the sudden loss of every person who has ever loved them, constant hunger, emotional destruction, sexual abuse, and a violence that is unrelenting. Pressed into lives of perpetual danger, they find that it takes all their energy just to survive. They live with a daily fear of their own impending death for the slightest mistake. They are dehumanized and made into commodities— not mere objects, but objects programmed to kill.

And yet, out of the horror of these circumstances, courageous and resilient human beings can be born. I have found deep reserves of resiliency in each of the formerly abducted children that I have met. The triumph of that spirit has saved them from despair on countless occasions. A twelve-year-old boy named Charles, just after his escape, told his family: "I was so afraid of dying. But my friends warned me that if the rebel commanders detected any fear in me they would kill me, so I had to pretend to be brave."

I saw an extraordinary strength of spirit in Agnes. After finishing high school she made a commitment to work for one year at a center in northern Uganda that helps counsel formerly abducted children who, like herself, have been thrown into war and are intimately familiar with its horrors. She could see herself in their current struggles to reclaim their lives from their kidnappers. Agnes has a wisdom and a social maturity that far exceed her years. She considers her belief in God to be her greatest source of strength. Her career aspiration is to study law, to become an advocate for the rights of others. She told me: "I don't regret that I was abducted, because now I understand the sufferings of others." Her life is a powerful witness to just how resilient the human spirit can be.

There were approximately fifty-five armed conflicts raging across our world in 2002 and children were employed in at least half of them. Astonishingly, there are approximately three hundred thousand child soldiers in our world, over one-third of them in the

Great Lakes region of Africa. Today children who have been forcibly separated from their families will be made to fight in deadly skirmishes in Sierra Leone, Cambodia, Pakistan, Burundi, Colombia, the Democratic Republic of Congo, El Salvador, Guatemala, Angola, Eritrea, Ethiopia, Rwanda, Sudan, Afghanistan, Liberia, Uganda, and elsewhere.

To many of us in North America, the senseless violence that destroys thousands of young lives seems exceedingly tragic but remote. It must be the concern of someone other than ourselves. Yet Sunday and Agnes are our children too; they belong to us. Whenever we allow a girl or boy anywhere on the earth to be reduced to a non-person, then one more thread is plucked out of the fabric that holds the human family together. Until our moral outrage joins with that of others around the world in demanding that this insanity stop, it is likely that Joseph Kony and others like him will continue to inflict untold suffering upon the most vulnerable of us all.

SEEKING THE GRACE OF NEW BEGINNINGS

The Hasidic rabbi Levi Yitzhak of the Ukraine is fond of telling friends of his visit to the Polish countryside. One evening the rabbi was visiting the owner of a tavern. As he walked in, he saw two peasants at a table. Both were drinking with reckless abandon, arms around each other, protesting how much each loved the other. Suddenly Ivan said to Peter: "Peter, tell me, what hurts me?" Bleary-eyed, Peter looked at Ivan: "How do I know what hurts you?" Ivan's answer was swift: "If you don't know what hurts me, how can you say you love me?"

Like Ivan, Archbishop John Baptist Odama, the Roman Catholic archbishop of Gulu, believes he needs to know the afflictions of his people if he is to serve them with the heart of Christ. The afflictions of his people are many. Life for most people in the Gulu district of northern Uganda is short, brutish, and entrenched in poverty. Archbishop Odama listens with attentive love to everyone he shepherds, but there is obviously a special place in his heart for young people. He delights in their company and finds himself drawn to them: their simplicity and spontaneity are irresistible. Having become innocent victims of so many forces beyond their control, they can make a special claim on his love and ministry.

In Gulu, along with the neighboring district of Kitgum, approximately 14,000 children were abducted from their families during the last ten years. Nearly all of them were kidnapped by the Lord's Resistance Army and many of them died during their captivity. A rare outbreak of the dreaded ebola virus struck Gulu from August 2000 until January 2001. It killed 173 people and orphaned some 475 children. Long before this outbreak, the HIV virus had already ravaged this community and its families, forcing a legion of children to face their future without parents to nurture and love them.

Disease and violence have long stalked the people of Gulu. They are among the crosses these distant people bear. Carrying a cross is not always an act of love, but it can always become one. Therefore, the ministry of Archbishop Odama includes the struggle to help his people transform sheer suffering into redemptive acts. Odama believes that only then will his people possess the power to bring forth a future born of hope. But he senses that, before he can become a guide for his people, he must first be their companion, a companion willing to share their suffering.

I had the opportunity to witness up close the actions of this remarkable minister of God's love. As he presided at early morning Mass one day in his small chapel, he asked me to proclaim the gospel. The passage was from Matthew, chapter 18, where Jesus is approached with the question: "Lord, when my brother wrongs me, how often must I forgive him?" While seated after the gospel, with his eyes remaining closed, the archbishop began to tell us the story of two boys he had met at Gusco Camp.

One of these boys had managed to escape the rebels after a year in captivity. Gusco Camp had been his new home for about two months before his return to his mother, his only living relative. The boy had felt safe at Gusco. It was there that he had begun to rebuild his life and experience some measure of contentment for the first time in a very long while. As the day of his departure approached, he grew restless and fearful. His newfound sense of security was rapidly dissipating.

After going home, he lived each day in a terrible fear of being re-abducted. Compounding this fear was the fact that he lived alone with his mother and felt that she could do very little to protect him. He had been kidnapped from home, so he knew that the rebels knew where to find him. The mother and son were far too poor to move away. Even with their lives at stake they remained vulnerable, rendered immobile by economic conditions.

One day, while digging in the garden next to his house, the boy noticed people approaching from a distance. It was the rebels coming to take him back. He immediately hid from view, but stayed close enough to watch and hear what would happen. He noticed that some of the rebels were child soldiers, just as he had been. The group demanded from the mother the whereabouts of her son. Her answer was protective and loving: "I have not seen my son since you took him from me over a year ago." The son, hiding in the nearby bushes, feared for his mother's safety but felt he could do nothing. He was too frightened to come out of hiding. One of the rebel leaders ordered a boy under his command to kill the mother for not speaking the truth to him. As the son watched helplessly from his hiding place, he saw the other boy beat his mother to death.

Several days after his mother's funeral, having nowhere else to go, this boy begged the staff at Gusco to open their hearts to him and let him stay at the camp. They agreed to this, at least as an interim measure, and Gusco once more became his home. Several weeks later, a large raid on the LRA forces freed many child soldiers who had been abducted. They all came to Gusco, and among them was the boy who had killed the other boy's mother.

When the boys first saw each other at the camp, neither one could believe his eyes. Fate had brought them together. One boy immediately confronted the other: "You are the one who killed my mother—I saw you do it!" The accused child denied it vehemently, but his accuser detailed every action, every word spoken. God's grace then touched the hearts of both boys. Soon both of them were crying, faced by a truth that was so clear and so exceedingly painful. Truth and forgiveness met in that decisive moment. One boy was given the courage to face an awful truth; the other was given the grace to forgive the worst thing anyone could have done to him.

Archbishop Odama tells us in his homiletic reflection that this is what it means to transform sheer suffering into a redemptive act. And it will be children like these who will show us the way.

All that separated that young boy from being re-abducted by the rebels was his mother's unyielding courage and her desire to live for him. She alone became the shield that protected her son from the brutality that threatened to engulf his life once more. She upheld the sacred trust that the youngest generation places in their elders to do for them what they cannot do for themselves.

That mother's sacrificial surrender of her life can also be seen as a cry to all of us who live in this world's relatively secure and safe environments. It is a cry of a very particular kind. It appeals for a far-sightedness that is able to recognize the precariousness and the vulnerability of others whose suffering remains at a distance from our own. Perhaps it is akin to what Fyodor Dostoyevsky meant when, in *The Brothers Karamazov*, he said: "We are all guilty of all and for all men before all, and I more than the others."[2] Every one of the conversations and encounters that I have had with former child soldiers has left me with a subtle, gnawing, and bewildering sense of guilt.

As I listened to former child soldiers tell me about how adults forced them to kill other children or to cut off another child's arm or leg solely because that child was slow, or stubborn, or sick, it was impossible for me to escape feeling some responsibility for the horrific ordeals inflicted on them. One teenager told me that another boy his age was killed by a rebel leader for simply eating meat on a day when they had been ordered not to. Some of the children were commanded to smear themselves with the blood of those who had been slain. Random cruelty is a way of life in the rebel group. The emotional scars from all this must penetrate their young psyches with incredible force, and this at a time in life when a child or teenager would naturally expect to be protected by the adult world, not brutalized by it.

Going home for child soldiers is seldom easy. For some formerly abducted adolescents like Joyce, a nineteen-year-old mother of two, the return has been marked by an overwhelming sorrow. She was forced to spend most of her teenage years with the LRA. Eventually she became a possession of a top leader and bore a child by him. When she managed to escape with her daughter, she returned directly to the village in which she had spent her childhood. She was utterly surprised when her former boyfriend accepted her back into his life. For a time they lived together and even had a child of their own. Joyce contends that her boyfriend's male friends persuaded him that he had been wrong to accept her. She overheard them telling him that abducted girls are not normal, that they are "damaged people." He soon turned her and the children out of the house.

Joyce now lives alone with her children and spends most of the day digging to cultivate food for her small children. She tells me she fears for the future and wonders how long she can hold things together. Her look is weary; she stares into space, unable to make sense of her life. As she tells me her story, I am reminded of how those involved directly with providing counsel and aid to former child soldiers have told me that it is especially difficult for girls who have been sexually abused while in captivity to be reintegrated into the community. Some sectors in society can be especially unforgiving of them.

ALLIANCES FOR THE PROTECTION OF CHILDREN

The image of the young boy's mother standing alone against the rebels haunts me. I am a part of the world of responsible adults who possess the power to be advocates in solidarity with those whose rights have been violated and who cannot defend themselves. Children and women are especially vulnerable in times of armed conflict and upheaval. They are frequently targeted by warring groups seeking to spread a reign of terror. I had not realized before now the inhuman conditions into which children are thrown whenever guerrilla warfare rages. They are the prime targets, the fresh recruits who will be forced to surrender everything for a cause they are far too young even to understand.

At the time this mother was murdered for protecting her son from the LRA, these same rebels who were killing innocent people with impunity were receiving direct support from the government of Sudan. The Sudanese government justified this action by stating that Uganda had allegedly been supporting the Sudanese People's Liberation Army (SPLA), a rebel group seeking to overthrow Sudan's government in Khartoum. Tragically, two nations in an adversarial relationship with each other were willing to let children's lives be destroyed in a political quagmire created by people in power.

Those who commit atrocities against children are not immune from the political forces in our world. We all have a responsibility to mobilize effective political action within our national communities to protect children everywhere from the horrors and effects of armed conflict. At the urging of Els De Temmerman, the author of *Aboke Girls*, members of the European Parliament visited northern Uganda and met personally with formerly abducted children who have escaped the LRA. Upon their return to Europe they became the voices of those children to the European community. In August 2001, under intense political pressure to stop all support to the LRA, Sudanese president Omar El Bashir announced that his government had cut all its ties to the rebel forces under the command of Joseph Kony. With this action the prospects for peace were enhanced and fresh hope was given to a swifter end to child abduction in this region of the world.

Vastly broadened alliances between groups of people investing themselves in the security of the world's children are a vital and effective way to counter foes like the LRA and other rebel forces. One of the greatest ethical challenges of our day is to knit together a common front, a global safety net capable of ensuring that children everywhere can grow up in an environment free from violence.

How can we harmonize our longing for domestic peace with love for someone in danger across the globe? Finding an answer to this daunting question is all the more urgent as a protracted, global war on terrorism rages with no end in sight. The struggle for a world set free from senseless, vengeful violence has entered a new day. In this new era, the interconnectedness of all those forces that spur violence are suddenly seen with greater clarity. We can sense in a fresh way how abject poverty breeds despair and despair breeds terrorism. It is no surprise then that Afghanistan, voted by the respected *Economist* magazine in 2001 as the worst place on earth to live, was the breeding ground for the most horrific terror ever unleashed against the United States.

Across the globe, local governments, bands of concerned citizens, and religious communities are often the first line of protection for children at risk of violence. While traveling very close to the border of Sudan and Uganda I was a guest in the home of Comboni missionaries in the village of Opit. I arrived late at night, but a warm meal and gracious company awaited me and my traveling companions. Early the next morning I went with the pastor, Father Ponziano Velluto, to unlock the church for the first Mass. It was still dark and I assumed we were alone in the church. Suddenly I saw shadows of figures rising from the ground and all about us there was a sudden sense of movement. Little ones were slowly getting up from their mats and older children were carrying things for the younger ones as everyone filed out of the church. I was startled to learn that more than 120 children had been sleeping on the floor of this parish church every night for months. It is the most secure building in the village and the place where the children feel safest. Some of them had several miles to walk to get home for breakfast, but they had been given a secure night's rest, a treasure not to be taken for granted in this region of the world.

The band of concerned citizens known as the Grandmothers of the Plaza de Mayo in Buenos Aires is a prime example of action taken to protect children today. The grandmothers no longer search only for their own family members. They carry placards that read: "All youngsters with doubts about their true identity, come to us, we will be waiting for you with love in order to help you!" That message, backed up by their determination to make a difference in the lives of at-risk children, makes them an example to the world of the kind of advocacy that can help bring all our children into a brighter tomorrow.

In June,1998, six international non-governmental organizations (NGOs)—Amnesty International, the Jesuit Refugee Service, the Quaker United Nations Office, the International Federation of Terre des Hommes, Human Rights Watch, and the International Save the Children Alliance—joined together to form the Coalition to Stop the Use of Child Soldiers. At the strong urging of this new coalition, and with massive support from other agencies working with children, the United Nations General Assembly adopted an Optional Protocol to the Convention on the Rights of the Child in May 2000. Prior to this new protocol, the minimum age for compulsory recruitment into military service by any government had been set at fifteen. The Optional Protocol raises the minimum age to eighteen and also prohibits recruitment of anyone under the age of eighteen by non-governmental forces. In May 2002 the UN Security Council directed Kofi Annan to submit to it a list of all known conflicts in our world that employ minors in armed combat. Mr. Annan declared that the time of lamenting the use of child soldiers is over. It is now time to hold accountable and to punish those who wage, legitimize, and support wars and rebel insurgencies that systematically recruit children to fight and kill. The political inertia that has allowed armed conflict to wreak havoc on the lives of countless children is now being confronted as never before.

In war-afflicted regions of our world, international NGOs such as World Vision are engaged in providing medical care, nutritional rehabilitation, psycho-social support, and ongoing counseling to war-traumatized children. With their education having been interrupted by war, these young people are often anxious to go back to school. Older children are also eager for vocational training. Marketable skills in the Great Lakes region of Africa include bicycle repair, tailoring, carpentry, and farming.

There is a also a moral imperative to minister to the families of the abducted children. These families have borne the brunt of the war's pain. They are certainly suffering intense loss as their abducted sons and daughters, brothers and sisters, are suddenly ripped from them and thrown into war.

One teenage boy, feeling overwhelming remorse at the loss of his sister abducted by the LRA in 1997, wrote a poem to express his outrage at war and those who perpetrate it. His words express the feelings of thousands of families:

The Blood-Thirsty Northern Ugandan War

For the last sixteen years you have been with us without
    invitation
The Lord's Resistance Army (LRA).
In the districts of Gulu, Kitgum, Pader, Lira, Apac, and
    the surrounding districts of Northern Uganda,
Leaving our loved ones to wail and toil for the next day,
    helplessly,
With sleepless nights spent in the bush for fear of dear life
Under the blistering cold and the mosquitoes.
Our young brothers and sisters have been forcefully
    abducted for recruitment to fight—
Fight a war they do not understand.
They are indoctrinated and dehumanized into killing
    machines.
Is this what the Lord's Army should be doing?
Forced to kill their parents and relatives so they do not
    want to come back,
They are taken into captivity to live in the bush like wild
    animals,
Forced to drink human blood and urine like animals of the
    jungle.
The war in Northern Uganda.
You have left our loved ones maimed by landmines.
We have lost our loved ones to death because of you.
Thousands of our young brothers and sisters have dis-
    appeared into forced captivity, never to be seen again.

Development has become a word of the past to us because
    of you, the Northern War.
Haven't you claimed enough lives and drunk enough
    blood?
How many more do you still want to claim?
The dream of the perpetrators of this war is our night-
    mare.
Is this bloodthirsty Northern Ugandan war still a "civil
    war" or is it terrorism?
Our brothers and sisters forcefully abducted—we still
    love you and want you back unconditionally!
Can the whole world come to our rescue and find a solu-
    tion for a lasting peace in Northern Uganda?
Do we appreciate the sight of a child suckling the breasts
    of its dead mother—
Like the one in the Acoli Pii Refugee Camp massacre?
If we do not find a lasting solution to this war, then soon
    the whole of Northern Uganda will be suckling
    breasts of its dead mothers.
Please, peace-loving members of this earth, hear the cries
    of the children and people of Northern Uganda and
    come to our help.
Otherwise generations are being wiped out!

Dedicated to my beloved sister abducted in 1997
WE LOVE AND MISS YOU

THE STEPS TOWARD HEALING

Psychologists who have worked with former child soldiers suggest that acquiring a new and deep sense of belonging is the most
crucial component to a successful reintegration process. Even
though life will never be the same for these children and teenagers, even though there simply is no returning to the lives they
knew before abduction, there can be healing. The forging of new
experiences of trust and friendship which strengthen the ties that

bind them to their families, loved ones, and peers will gradually allay many of the fears that have engulfed their young lives, especially the fear that they are no longer worthy of love.

Unfortunately, freedom often means exposure to new negative experiences. Some former child soldiers are stigmatized through name-calling and ridicule, often coming from their peers, whose acceptance they crave. Former child soldiers have heightened fears and are extraordinarily sensitive to any perceived sense of mistrust or avoidance. Their normal emotional development has been arrested as a result of the utter brutality they have known. Many feel strange and out of place in the world to which they have returned. They naturally envy their peers who have been blessed with years of nurture by the adult world while they were robbed of their childhood. Knowing themselves to be different from their peers, they find the challenge of forming new friendships exceedingly daunting. Anxiety can even lead a few to ask, "Why did I come back?"

In the first weeks of Agnes's freedom, her parents frequently told her that they didn't love her like they used to love her—they loved her more now than before the ordeal of her abduction. They explained to her that they now knew precisely how empty their home would be if they were to lose her forever.

Nowhere has the practice of using children in warfare been more widespread and repulsive than in Sierra Leone. Commanders in that nation's most notorious rebel group, the Revolutionary United Front, terrorize children abducted into their rebel cause by branding them like cattle with their army's initials, RUF. The object is to stigmatize the children. The permanent marks, usually cut with a knife into their chests, show the world who they belong to and where their allegiance lies. Sometimes the letters are cut right into the children's foreheads so they become like giant billboards. The shame of bearing this mark has led some of the children to pour acid on their bodies in futile attempts to remove or cover the mark. It is a mark meant to send a message to all who see it: I am the property of rebel soldiers, and my life is not my own.

Dr. Jeff Colyer, a plastic surgeon from Kansas City who volunteers with America's International Medical Corps, has surgically removed these marks for scores of children in Sierra Leone and has taught local African doctors how to do the procedure. He wishes he could remove the emotional and spiritual scars that run as deep as the knife wounds, but he knows that he cannot. Still, the young people are always elated when the dreaded mark is removed. Dr. Colyer cherishes the moment when the bandages are first drawn back after the operation. These children who have long avoided looking at their chests now stare at their own bodies in delight. It is a moment of grace.

Unconditional forgiveness and reconciliation with family and community remain the only healing avenue toward new life for former child soldiers. Sadly, however, this gift is sometimes withheld. It often happens that these extremely young war-survivors feel guilty just for being alive. And the spiral of their personal destruction continues unabated as certain governments make the terrible choice to hold them responsible for what has happened to them while they were caught up in guerrilla warfare. Why? Because the unjust adult aggressors who have wreaked untold violence against them elude capture. So, unable to punish the adults who abducted these vulnerable youngsters and transformed their lives into nightmares, governments punish the children.

In a number of countries, Colombia being a pre-eminent example, the judicial system criminalizes and detains child soldiers. These children will, in all likelihood, be imprisoned and punished for the very evils inflicted upon them. Once removed from the rebel groups, they are victimized further and their alienation as outcasts is extended. What does this say about the moral solidarity we claim to possess with victims of unspeakable crimes?

AMERICANS AWAKENING TO HOW WAR WOUNDS CHILDREN

On December 5, 2001, the U.S. Department of State placed the rebel group Lord's Resistance Army on its list of known terrorist operatives. By this time, the complacency and silence surrounding the use of children in warfare, in rebel movements and terror groups had already begun to be broken.

The tragic attacks on the U.S. homeland waged by Al Qaeda on September 11, 2001, changed America forever, especially the way Americans understand their security. Some have begun to wonder if it might also have transformed our moral landscape. It has been suggested that there was created that day a new, mass-scale willingness to touch the pain that exists outside American soil.

Photos of twelve-year-old boys, Taliban fighters carrying semi-automatic weapons, became familiar images to millions of U.S. citizens who previously had been unaware of the reality of children in warfare. They were exposed to information on millions of children in war-weary lands living daily with the weight of fear. It is a fear to which Americans could now relate in a startlingly new and most personal way. Our nation had been struck by a violent evil; we found ourselves unable to protect our loved ones. Americans began to become aware that this is a reality being played out in many, many places across the globe.

In such regions as the Middle East, parts of Africa, Asia, and Central America, large numbers of people are routinely afraid to leave their homes on account of the land mines, random attacks, or bombings that constantly plague their neighborhoods. Among the most fearful are the children who hesitate to leave home for school because of potential threats to their safety.

The students at Pittsburgh Central Catholic High School learned of the plight of the child soldiers of Gusco from reading articles in *America* magazine. They wanted to do something concrete to be in solidarity with them. They contacted the director of the camp for war-traumatized children and asked his advice. His first suggestion was that the Pittsburgh students make a video recording and send their personal messages to their counterparts in East Central Africa. They did so. Their concern helped the African child soldiers know that they did not stand all alone in this world, that there were other young people their own age who knew of their plight and who cared.

An incredible drama of overwhelming emotional impact opened on the stage of the George Mason University's Theater of the First Amendment in Washington, D.C., on December 5, 2002. *Children of War* tells the story of five young people victimized by war. Its author, Ping Chong, portrays the stories of these Washington-area immigrants who range in age from twelve to eighteen. They fled the terror in their homelands of El Salvador, Sierra Leone, Kurdistan, Somalia, and Afghanistan. As the children tell their own personal stories on the stage, it becomes evident that their spirits remain deeply bruised. They carry hidden emotional and physical scars that may not be easy to detect. Still, by the end of the presentation, everyone knows the hell these children have experienced.

NOTES

1. Els De Temmerman, *Aboke Girls: Children Abducted in Northern Uganda* (Kampala: Fountain Publishers, 2001).

2. Fyodor Dostoyevsky, *The Brothers Karamazov*, trans. Constance Garnett (New York: New American Library, 1957), 264.

2
Slow Death by Exploitation

Bourbon Street in the heart of the French Quarter in New Orleans pulsates with life as crowds of tourists revel in the spirit of the city known as the "Big Easy." Jazz fills the air, alcohol flows freely, and everywhere there is something interesting to purchase. But there is a dark side to this celebrated street.

At night, scantily dressed teenagers of both sexes stand on the sidewalks leading into the French Quarter. Some call them "runaway" kids, but they are more likely "throwaway" kids. Certainly at sixteen and seventeen years of age they are far too young to fully comprehend the personal destruction that accompanies mixing sex and money at any age. Unknown to them, they have become unwitting victims of a sex-drenched culture that will one day discard them. Regrettably, for some of them, much that is worth living for will have been lost before they realize what has happened.

New Orleans is one of America's most popular tourist destinations. It is a vibrant city that shouts to the world "Let the good times roll!" Few may even notice that when poverty and tourism meet, the end result often is the sexual exploitation of the young and vulnerable. Indeed, there is a marked increase in the flagrant sale and trafficking of adolescents worldwide, most especially in cities and resort locations that have the reputation of being tourist magnets.

How does one begin to tell the sad story? Seductively dressed young people lurk at the entrance to the French Quarter every night. Many of these young people may have attempted earlier in the day to sell their plasma for fifteen dollars, or they might have

Judy Walgren, The Photo Project/India. Used with permission.

Men's eyes follow a young prostitute
canvassing a street in India.

shoplifted to feed the cravings brought on by addiction. Now they will subtly offer the impression to passers-by that they are "available." A glance is exchanged, an understanding arrived at, a price paid.

For the last three decades Congresswoman Lindy Boggs, the former U.S. ambassador to the Holy See, has made the French Quarter her home. From her balcony overlooking Bourbon Street she can nightly see the parade of humanity pass by. Among the throngs of people on the crowded streets below are many young people—some only in their late teens—who have become addicted to crack and whose lives are being slowly consumed by the desperate search for the next crack fix. Crack is a chemically purified crystallized form of cocaine that is highly addictive and readily available on the streets of major cities in the United States. Ambassador Boggs tells me that it is precisely this combination of the drug's availability and its highly addictive nature that she fears makes it one of the worst of all possible enemies to young people on the streets.

Some of the young people on the streets of New Orleans will find a way out of this nightmarish cycle of addiction and prostitution. Their chance at a new life often comes through a grace they encounter at Covenant House, the largest system of shelters for street kids across the U.S., Canada, and Latin America. The Covenant House network has become a powerful advocate for adolescents caught up in desperate situations. Every young person who lives on the streets of New Orleans knows the Covenant House address—611 N. Rampart Street. It is a well-known safe haven to youth who have come to realize that they need help to escape the destruction of life on the streets.

Teenagers who live on streets sleep in the hidden alleys of major cities all across the United States. They can be found in abandoned cars and buildings, on park benches, under bridges and freeway overpasses. Behind their know-it-all-I'm-not-afraid-of-anyone-or-anything attitude, they are fearful of the treacherous streets they call home. They are alone, frequently despondent, hungry, and—most of all—desperate to find someone who cares.

They experience all the predictable troubles one might expect in the lives of teenagers attempting to raise themselves: abuse, malnutrition, addiction, despair.

As president of Covenant House, Sister Mary Rose McGeady has emerged as a leading front-line expert on the sexual exploitation of young people on America's streets. She has more sad stories to tell about at-risk kids than anyone I have ever met. Some of the stories seem unbelievable.

David, a sixteen-year-old boy who sought shelter at Covenant House in New York, once approached Sister Mary Rose with an odd question: "Sister, how much do you get paid to take care of me?" As is so frequently the case, there was a meaning to his words that remained hidden just below the surface. With extraordinary tact, Sister Mary Rose probed for the underlying reason why this teenager seemed so interested in her finances. He began to open up to her and she learned that just before David's mother threw him out of the family home, she had been bemoaning the fact that the state paid her money for each foster child she took in. If David were gone, she would be able to replace him with a foster child who generated income. "She told me to get out," David said to Sister Mary Rose. "She said she wasn't making any money on me. I'm her son! She said those other kids were worth more than me. Can you believe that, Sister?"

Sadly, Sister Mary Rose could believe it. In over fifty-five years of ministry as a Daughter of Charity of St. Vincent de Paul, she has far too often seen how children can be treated like "little living and breathing commodities," even by those entrusted with their care, people whom we would expect to encircle them with their own protective love. Instead, family members, and even parents, use and abuse these children as if they were disposable things.

While David's anger on the outside was clearly directed at his mother, no doubt inside there were more personal demons to face, unanswered questions about himself. One of the questions Sister Mary Rose is frequently asked by homeless children and adolescents is: "What did I do to deserve this?" Deep inside, wracked with feelings of self-loathing and unworthiness, young people who are abandoned fear that they are not worthy of love. Even those who are not abandoned, those who run away from families that have attempted to reach out to them, can be plagued by self-doubt, somehow feeling that they deserve to be all alone in this world. The fear and self-doubt they carry make them extremely hesitant to trust any other human being.

Their profound feelings of self-doubt are sometimes generated by sexual conflicts. Sister Mary Rose once told me that I would be shocked if I knew how many teenage boys had been thrown out of their homes once their parents had come to believe that their sons had a homosexual orientation. The hostility directed at them by their own parents for something beyond their power to control can leave wounds that never heal. Shame and negativity, especially if they originate with those we love and trust the most, are easily internalized. Self-hatred has driven countless gay teens to act out in destructive ways. A study conducted by an agency of the U.S. government recently reported that homosexual youth are three times more likely than their peers to commit suicide. This terrible fact, while shocking, is understandable in light of the absolute rejection these teens experience.

Many teens who are either confused or disturbed by their emerging sexuality may choose the false sense of independence that life on the streets appears to offer. They opt for the streets as the place where they can get through this turbulent time in their lives. They sense a need to "ride it out alone." Ironically, this is one of those crucial junctures in life when they need all the nurture and guidance that responsible adults who love them could provide. Some of these teenagers will not survive a single year on the street. Suicide, homicide, drug overdoses, and other tragic acts will end their young lives.

There are some folks who are giving everything they can to see that these at-risk youths do survive. At Covenant House in New Orleans I met a middle-aged, married man named Rick Risher from Dothan, Alabama. Rick is a retired Army helicopter pilot, turned successful businessman, turned advocate for our nation's "disposable youth." At night, Rick is part of an outreach team that goes out in search of the young people whom we have thrown away. Team members go out with sandwiches, clean underwear, new socks, and a genuine desire to communicate. And what is their message? It is direct, disarming, and undeniable: "We need each other." Underlying the message is the belief that there are bonds that link all of us to each other in wondrous, mysterious ways. For the young people who can begin to accept this message, it comes as life-saving news.

Young People Bought and Sold

There is a slow death by exploitation for the street kids of the U.S.A. By contrast, on the other side of the globe, in the provincial city of Ubon Ratchitani in northeastern Thailand, a young girl named Siri languishes in a nightmare that is immediate. The very first night she was in debt-bondage, at age fifteen, she was shocked to discover that she would be required to have sex with a minimum of fifteen men per night. She felt a terrible soreness in her body. Her spirit was torn apart as a growing realization of and resignation to her dark future took hold of her. Now she prays daily to Buddha to spare her from HIV infection.

In a book documenting contemporary forms of slavery, *Disposable People: The New Slavery in the Global Economy,*[1] the British scholar Kevin Bales offers a penetrating look at the commercial sex industry in Thailand, of which Siri is one sad part. He narrates how thousands of young girls there are sold into slavery by their own parents. The parents may be told that their daughters are going to work in factories or in private homes of the wealthy as cooks and maids, but they suspect other possibilities. The money generated by placing a young person in debt-bondage is often used by parents to purchase food, medicine, and education for the remaining children. There is also the lure of expensive consumer items like an air conditioner, a car, a refrigerator, or a rice cooker.

Professor Bales relates the story of how Siri was sold in 1998 for $2,000, a very substantial amount of money for her family of rice farmers.

As unimaginable as this is for us, as utterly shocking and remote from our experience as this exchange appears, it is the international sex tourism industry that makes it possible. In other words, as much as we would like to believe that we have nothing to do with this abominable act, we do. It has been documented that five million unaccompanied men visited Thailand in 1996; large numbers of these men were sex tourists. Western European and American travelers joined in these ventures. Perhaps we ought to be very cautious in pointing to our society's moral rectitude when, in fact, we have contributed directly to what is most exploitative of the young in Thailand.

The global sex tourism industry flourishes in our day because there is such a strong market for the merchandising of children and women. The dehumanizing practices that surround this industry not only reduce its victims to sexual commodities but also demean the lives of all women and children. Sex tourism further perpetuates male chauvinism and the ongoing inequalities between the sexes. What happens in Thailand influences what happens in the United States, in New Orleans, in New York City, in our local towns. While the Thai government has adopted new official statutes that appear to be protecting the vulnerable youth who are so sought after by the sex industry, neither law nor conscience has been very effective in restricting this kind of exploitation. Why? Because of money.

It is impossible to accurately document how vast a flow of money enters Thailand's fragile economy through sex tourism, but experts place it in the billions. Astonishingly, sex tourism is many times more lucrative than the manufacturing and exporting of computers, a leading industry in this region of Southeast Asia. It is estimated that approximately $300 million is transferred annually from urban to rural areas in Thailand by women and girls working in the sex trade. This amount represents a small fraction of the total paid for the sexual services of the women and girls. The majority of the profit goes to others. Yet no amount of money could ever replace the dignity lost by the girls and women involved.

According to the International Organization for Migration, the smuggling of children and women for the purpose of sexual exploitation is one of the fastest growing branches of organized crime. Trafficking in arms and drugs in most countries poses greater risks for prosecution than trafficking in humans. Illegal drugs receive greater attention in the legal system than women and children. The most alluring factor to criminals is that children and women forced into commercial sex can be sold over and over again. One brothel owner remarked: "Once a drug is sold, it's gone, but a girl can be sold over and over before she collapses, goes mad, commits suicide, or dies of disease." His words foretell the sad end of far too many young lives.

In recent years, Central America has become more and more a place of sex tourism and exploitation of young people by tourists desirous of anonymous sexual encounters. Resort locations throughout Central America teem with young people for sale nearly everywhere. On any given day, at least two thousand juveniles can be found scraping out an existence on the streets of Costa Rica's capital city, San José.

During the last decade Mexico has also witnessed explosive growth in the child pornography industry. Mexico City, with the largest population of any city in the world, may have as many as two million young people raising themselves, many of them on the streets. Hunger and loneliness are the only constant companions for many of these vulnerable children and adolescents. They often seek a temporary reprieve from the harshness of life on the streets by sniffing glue. Their drug of choice is shoe glue, a solvent-based narcotic that is cheap and easily available. According to UNICEF, there are forty million street children in Latin America, and more than half of them regularly inhale solvent-based glues. Without parental supervision and nurture, without caring adults in their lives to protect and guide them, these children are the first to fall victim to sexual exploitation by adults.

In prostitution and pornography, the end result is the same. Young people are robbed of life, held like animals, bought and sold, and ultimately discarded if they contract a sexually transmitted disease. At that point, they can no longer be used like commodities for the sexual pleasure of adults. Amazingly little attention has been given to this because those who fall victim are the children of the poor and the defenseless, or, in other words, disposable people.

Casa Alianza, the Latin American sister-agency of the Covenant House movement in North America, has fearlessly stood up against the powerful sex-tourism industry growing in this region of the world. It appears to be a very dangerous task to speak up for our world's "throwaway" children. Casa Alianza's shelter for young people in Guatemala City has been threatened, attacked, and sprayed with machine-gun fire. One leader of the Casa Alianza movement, Bruce Harris, has received repeated death threats.

Casa Alianza has been one of the chief chroniclers of the growing phenomenon of child prostitution and pornography throughout Central America, often involving children as young as seven years old. It has collaborated with the Federal Bureau of Investigation and other U.S. agencies to uncover the identities of those Americans who have traveled abroad in order to prey upon young children who do not have the legal minimal protections that children in the U.S. have. According to Title 18, Section 2423, now a federal statute in the United States, it is a crime for any American citizen to travel abroad with the intent of sexually abusing children.

Still, many adults who participate in the sex-tourism industry do not consider their actions with children to be predatory or abusive. Sexual abusers use various excuses to exonerate themselves. They spin a web of self-deception. They tell themselves that the child is already a prostitute; that this is the life the child has chosen; that the money they are paying is desperately needed and will help feed this young person and others; that there are freer mores in foreign countries where young people become more sexually experienced at an earlier age and so it is more natural and less shameful for everyone involved.

In fact, children who engage in sexual activity with adults do not do so because they live in societies with freer mores, but precisely because they are not free. They are not free in two distinct, though interconnected ways: first, they are made captive by sexual coercion or, more literally, sexual slavery; and second, they are also captive by virtue of their youth, their lack of a fully developed capacity for choice.

Children and adolescents are frequently forced into sexual experiences with adults by circumstances beyond their control. They are coerced, tricked, or abducted; often they are fleeing situations of violent abuse or criminal neglect. Many of these young people are left with permanent scars, with accompanying feelings of low self-esteem and an unhealthy perspective on sexuality. Their prospects for happy, wholesome lives are very slim.

Processes associated with the globalization of the economy have aggravated the problem of human trafficking. In their increasingly desperate search for better living conditions, women and children living in situations of abject poverty fall prey to traffickers. The countries of origin of these women and children are predominantly the poorest nations and regions of our world as well as areas of economic transition or war. A disproportionately great number of women are trafficked from African countries, especially Ethiopia, Gambia, Zambia, Nigeria, South Africa, Togo, and the Democratic Republic of Congo. Their destination is often Middle Eastern countries such as Bahrain, Saudi Arabia, or the United Arab Emirates as well as Europe and North America. Some are simply trafficked to other African countries. An estimated fifteen thousand Nigerian women have been trafficked for prostitution into Italy alone and perhaps as many as fifty thousand Nigerian women are sexually exploited across Europe.

In recent years there has been a similar explosive increase in human trafficking in Latin America. An estimated fifty thousand women from the Dominican Republic alone have been drawn into the commercial sex industry and are living outside their country.

This is the fourth highest number in the world, surpassed only by Thailand, Brazil, and the Philippines. As political and economic conflicts escalate in Colombia, greater numbers of women and children have become vulnerable to trafficking. They flee their homelands in search of opportunities and, regrettably, end up victims of forced labor and sexual exploitation.

THE EXCHANGE OF SEX FOR FOOD, MEDICINE, EDUCATION

In February 2002 the United Nations High Commissioner for Refugees reported that children in refugee camps in West Africa were being targeted for sexual exploitation. Locally hired camp officials were demanding sex in exchange for the medicine and food they were delivering to the camps. During a forty-day mission in October and November 2001, UN officials visited refugee camps in Sierra Leone, Liberia, and Guinea. Over fifteen hundred children and adults were interviewed. Many of the children reported that they thought giving in to sexual demands was the only option they had if they wanted to receive the food and medicine that was being delivered for them. Most of the abused children were girls whose ages were from thirteen to eighteen. The abusers frequently targeted children who were in the camps without their parents. One adolescent girl in Liberia told UN officials: "It's difficult to escape the trap of those people; they use food as bait to get you to have sex with them." The scars from this tragic experience are indelibly marked on her and others like her.

While adolescents caught up in prostitution in the United States may be desperate for money to pay for drugs, in some other parts of our world young people sell their bodies so as not to starve. Could there be any hope for such youngsters? Fortunately, there are some courageous and altruistic people who are attempting to reach out to them with love and care. One of Japan's most popular television personalities today is Tetsuko Kuroyanagi, who, since 1984, has served as a UNICEF goodwill ambassador. She has visited fourteen countries in twelve years in order to chronicle the conditions of our world's most unfortunate children.

In 1995 she traveled to Port-au-Prince, Haiti. While there she visited a cemetery notorious for being a place of child prostitution. Both young girls and boys were available for hire. A twelve-year-old girl named Nicole attempted to sell herself to the cameraman who was filming a documentary with the ambassador. Her price was 40 cents. When asked if she knew that she could get AIDS this way, she thought for a moment and then matter-of-factly answered: "I am afraid. But even if I get AIDS, I'll live a few years, won't I? You see, my family has no food for tomorrow."

When a caring adult offers to pay the school fees for a young student in Africa whose family is poor, it is considered a great blessing, an expression of solidarity. It often is a time of rejoicing and the emergence of the fresh promise of a better life. Unfortunately, in too many cases, an unspoken expectation lies hidden in the gift. The donor may actually be ingratiating himself with the family for the purpose of obtaining sexual favors.

Even teachers can become enemies of the education of young girls. Incidents of female students being coaxed or even coerced into sexual relations with teachers have been on the rise in Africa in recent years. According to a recent report by the Forum for African Women Educationalists (FAWE), 43.9 percent of the girls in upper primary and secondary schools drop out of school as a result of pregnancy. Many African educators now privately admit that more and more teachers are joining the ranks of those responsible for this alarming number of pregnancies.

One AIDS worker, Jabulani Siwela, struggling to help stem the tide of AIDS infections in Zimbabwe, frequently saw teacher-student sex in the high school he served. He often heard girls bragging to peers about having slept with a teacher. Sadly, many of these girls often remained in the dark about the dangers to which they had exposed themselves. They simply sought the badge of superiority they believed they had earned for having garnered the affections of a person of power, not realizing that they may have been infected with one of the world's most dangerous viruses. Jabulani Siwela notes: "The teachers are the worst. These are men who know better, but they still do it all the time."

The Widespread Sexual Abuse of the Young and the Dangers of Cybersex

Child sexual abuse is an evil that has long been with us, but it has been hidden. Its pervasiveness and the depth of the wounds it inflicts became clearer to many in 2001. As the clergy sexual abuse crisis in the American Catholic Church exploded, this most sensitive of topics became a matter of open and public discussion.

A far greater number of children suffer the effects of child sexual abuse than is generally assumed. Studies conducted by Father Stephen Rossetti and other experts in the field of human sexuality suggest that about one out of every three or four girls and one out of every five to eight boys in our society are sexually abused by the age of eighteen.[2] The staggering statistics of the numbers of young people who are forcefully exploited reminds us that we live in a violently sexualized culture.

There is no way to describe adequately the evil of such acts, the devastation of soul that is inflicted upon children and adolescents by sexual abuse. When moral, psychological, and sexual boundaries are transgressed by adults who are in privileged positions of trust with young people, the damage inflicted is radical and long-lasting. The victims of this kind of betrayal often carry into their future a disturbing sense of shame and a diminished capacity to trust anyone.

The Roman Catholic Church in the United States is now on the forefront in dealing with issues of bringing to light, treating, and preventing child sexual abuse in American society. In the last ten years the effort to help make our whole society safer for children has become a priority in many ecclesial communities, not only in the United States but throughout the world.

In 1996, in a small, quaint coastal town in Sicily, an energetic, middle-aged pastor named Father Fortunato Di Noto was serving the needs of his community in the parish of Madonna del Carmine when he made a grim discovery. He had been offering an Internet course to the children in his school, teaching them how to access the World Wide Web. The priest asked the youngsters to name some topics that they wanted to know more about. One little girl wanted to search for information about candy and suggested that they enter the word "lollipop" into the search engine. The priest typed in the word "slurpy," an Italian slang word for lollipop. Unknown to those in the classroom, this term can also be a vulgar, slang designation for a sex act. What appeared on the screen was a link to a group known as the Pedophile Liberation Front, an advocacy group for the pedophile lifestyle. A pedophile is defined as "an adult who has recurrent, intense, sexual urges and sexually arousing fantasies involving a prepubescent child."[3] (By comparison, adults drawn sexually toward adolescents are referred to as ephebophiles.) Beginning with this link, Father Fortunato uncovered a stream of Internet sites where messages addressed to children were posted. These letters sought to lure young people into sexual relationships with predatory adults.

With a single click of the mouse at his computer station, this Italian priest, a devoted teacher and mentor to the young, was instantly thrust into a dark corner of the universe that had been previously unimaginable to him. Here, caught up in this bewilderingly new and repulsive place, he was first startled and then enraged. He told a friend: "I'm lucky because I have faith. If I didn't, I'm sure I would have gone out there with a machine gun."

Father Fortunato was suddenly and painfully made aware that there exists a hellish, secret, global subculture in cyberspace where adults prey on children. He discovered websites where child rape is explicitly displayed and children are beaten and tortured for the viewing pleasure of adults. As unspeakable as all this may be, there is a worldwide market for such material, for images that would cause most people to turn away in profound revulsion.

Father Fortunato transformed his rage into moral action. He followed up with thousands upon thousands of web searches and, with a persistence that knew no bounds, he began to ferret out the originators of this offensive material. Knowing that young people are exposed to this kind of horrific debasement every time they go on line and that the personal lives and futures of many children are being destroyed daily by it, he simply never gave up. To this day he is still in pursuit of those who harm children this way. He has been so astute in tracing the trail linking distributors of child pornography and its users that law enforcement officers both in Europe and North America credit him with providing information leading to several breakthroughs in their investigations. He has been able to help investigators break international pedophile rings in Russia and the United States.

Father Fortunato entered a world most of us will never see— and that some refuse to acknowledge even exists. Some dare not admit, even to themselves, that within our own culture children can be so sexually brutalized and exploited. This priest-crusader laments: "The problem is that these kinds of things aren't very well known, and since they're not well known, people have a hard time believing them. Silence is what allows pedophiles to win." Is now the time for us to break the silence that protects them?

A national study conducted in the United States revealed that one in five children who go online regularly are approached by strangers for sex. The most common response among youngsters being preyed upon is silence. Fearful that a parent may cut off their access to the web, many young people simply do not tell their parents, or any other adults, about sexual propositions they receive over the Internet. They attempt to deal with offensive communications on their own.

The Internet is still in its infancy and its power for good and for ill is gradually being discovered. While computer technology has become a powerful vehicle for preying on potential victims, it is also an instrument that investigators can use in tracking the criminal activities of pedophiles and in gathering evidence against them. Vigilant parents can check the computer's bookmarks, cache, or history in order to monitor what their children are accessing.

Back in Italy, Father Fortunato continues his endless efforts to find and free all children who have become victims of online pedophilia. His ministry has taken on a new dimension he could never have predicted: unmasking the shameful, hidden ways in which society allows young people to suffer sexual violence. May his voice rally other voices to speak out loudly against this crime.

NOTES

1. Kevin Bales, *Disposable People: New Slavery in the Global Economy* (Berkeley, Calif.: University of California Press, 1999). See especially chap. 2, "Thailand: Because She Looks Like a Child."

2. Stephen Rossetti, *A Tragic Grace: The Catholic Church and Child Sexual Abuse* (Collegeville, Minn.: The Liturgical Press, 1996), 104.

3. Gerald D. Coleman, *Human Sexuality: An All-Embracing Gift* (New York: Alba House, 1992), 80.

3
Children Who Never Play

Carlos is ten years old. He is a Salvadoran boy who harbors a big dream. One day he wants to travel to North America where he expects to make a lot of money to send home to his mother and the rest of his family. But today he lives with the reality of being a breadwinner for them all. He knows he must start out for work by 5:00 in the morning. He has a short twenty-minute walk to the place where he will work till 6:00 in the evening.

Carlos has never gone to school. He and his older sister Antonia spend their days selling bags of water at a busy intersection on the main road from Chirilagua to San Miguel in El Salvador. Many buses stop here with thirsty people. This young boy is the second of five children born to his mother by three different men. None of these men supports their offspring financially or emotionally. Carlos has been forced to learn for himself what it means to grow up as a male in his family without a role model to emulate. Thus far, he has learned to manage money, to write his own name, and to live with distant dreams.

The mother of Carlos and Antonia stays at home cooking and taking care of the other children. She is completely dependent upon her son and daughter to bring home all that they earn, an average of four dollars a day. This is the sole source of livelihood for an entire family of six, a meager income that must go a very long way to purchase food and clothing for the whole family. As incredible as it is, the small earnings of children selling bags of water are what keep this family afloat.

Jon Warren, The Child Labor Photo Project. Used with permission.

Eleven-year-old Thavara searching for items to recycle in the main garbage dump of Phnom Penh, Cambodia.

Father Joe Callahan, an energetic young missionary from Ohio, has often had occasion to observe this boy at his workplace. He tells me that Carlos is the type of kid everyone enjoys being around; his fun-loving spirit is infectious. "He's very personable, very friendly, always smiling and joking with people. I've seen him doing this work for several years. He knows all the bus drivers and many of the passengers, and he'll often stay on the bus until the next stop and enjoy the ride. His life is hard, but that doesn't mean that he doesn't enjoy life." A brief bus ride, just a few moments long, can become the playful, fun moment of the day for Carlos.

They are often deliberately hidden from the public eye, yet children comprise a massive global workforce that the International Labor Organization estimates to be 250 million strong. They are children between the ages of five and fourteen who work for a living. Nearly 120 million of them work full time. The sight of young children forced to work instead of being engaged in the regular activities that should characterize childhood seems abhorrent to us. We know intuitively that schooling, play, nurture, and home activities in the company of family members and friends ought to characterize the daily experience of a child, one who is just beginning life, yet all too often children know only toil and labor.

Requiring children to work for hire is in direct violation of the moral pact we hold with our young. Our moral responsibility to the common good requires protecting them from whatever can stunt their growth and preparation, personal and intellectual, for life's future challenges. The daily monotony of engaging in menial and repetitive tasks and frequent exposure to harsh or even hazardous working conditions do away with any possibility of experiencing the pleasures and wondrous discoveries we commonly associate with being young. Perhaps societies tolerate exploitative child labor by simply pretending it does not exist. Too often child laborers are deliberately hidden from the public eye in the foolish belief that what we can successfully shield from view ought not to offend us.

Early on a Saturday morning I took a stroll through a small African village with the elderly pastor of the local parish. It was just after the first streaks of daylight had emerged and there was a sense of freshness everywhere. The very first persons we encountered on our walk were a family working in their garden. A young mother and father were working side by side with their three small children. I was a bit surprised to see a whole family hard at work at that early morning hour. I learned that the father was a teacher in the local school. The pastor commented to me: "These parents are an example to the whole community. It is a good witness for all of us in this village to see how they work together. A family bond is strengthened when the task of growing the family food is shared by all instead of being a burden for just a few. These children are in our school and excel under their mother's watchful care."

Seeing that family together in their garden reminded me of my own childhood years. When I was growing up, our family had a very large vegetable garden in the back yard and everyone in the family was expected to contribute to this effort. While it was work, it was also much more than work. It was an opportunity to come together as a family around a common purpose. It connected us to the earth and to each other.

My father prized the hours he was able to spend in the garden with his six sons. He subtly imparted his reverence for the earth to each of us. Being in the garden also meant being tutored by our parents on how seeds are planted and how new life emerges from those seeds hidden in the ground. Best of all, it was a way to invest ourselves in each other's well-being, since the produce from the garden would eventually help to feed our family and our neighbors. That was the fun of this family endeavor—taking the sweet corn, carrots, onions, tomatoes, and green beans to our friends. In my family home, at a very early age, I began to discover that work was part of the very rhythm of life. I also came to relish the joy of sharing the fruits of my work with others.

Child labor is vastly different from child work. Child labor jeopardizes the health, well-being, and education of young people.

It is forced labor extracted from those least able to provide it. In this sense it is closely akin to slavery, that form of coerced labor that has existed ever since human beings began to cultivate the land instead of hunting and gathering what grew in the wild.

The unjust practices that surround child labor, while widespread in our world, are most acute today in Asia, Africa, and Latin America. In Asia alone approximately 152 million children are exploited and abused through child labor. A common form of child labor in Pakistan is the manufacture of bricks. This work, like the work of a family in a garden, is often done alongside parents and siblings, but the nature, extent, and consequences of the children's involvement all point to its exploitative character.

The work of manufacturing bricks is inherently arduous and dangerous. The bricks are fired in kilns that can exceed 1500 degrees. Children who move and stack the hot bricks are always in danger of burns that both disfigure and disable. Just to be near the kilns is to be exposed to an unhealthy, oppressive heat. The workday begins with the mixing of water and soil, a task that normally starts at or before sunrise. Only in the heat of the day when temperatures soar and work must be suspended do children get the opportunity to eat and rest with their parents. In the cool of the late afternoon, work resumes until dark. The next day, the pattern is repeated. The work goes on as the children engage in the same repetitious and physically exhausting tasks day after day. Children in such situations come perilously close to becoming robots, faceless beings valued principally for what they can do.

The most devastating consequence is obvious: child laborers are not given the opportunities that would enable them to grow as persons, intellectually and emotionally. Children in a family of Pakistani brickmakers, if given the rare chance to attend a good school for even a short time, would make wondrous discoveries. They would find themselves, likely for the first time ever, in an atmosphere where the focus is on them, not on their work or their value to the family's survival. They might find it nearly incredible that their inner life, intellectual progress, imagination, and socialization skills truly mattered to the world of adults. If a child in a family of brickmakers in Pakistan is given the chance to receive some formal schooling, it is far more likely that the child will be a boy rather than a girl. Children who do not get the opportunity to be educated suffer significant disadvantages.

The emotional needs of child laborers are also neglected by the adult world. Children whose lives are given over to the most mundane tasks are routinely denied the time and attention needed to develop a sense of self-esteem and emotional attachments to family and friends. They know that energy is going out of them, but they experience very little energy returning in the form of emotional affirmation, joy, or delight.

The fact that child laborers are introduced to exploitative relationships very early on in life has profound, far-reaching consequences. Valued for what they do, not prized for who they are, they can naturally be expected to internalize the lesson that "the extent of your personal value is found in the extent of your usefulness." That message is conveyed in very subtle ways, but it is all-pervasive. Gradually child laborers can come to perceive all of life's relationships, even those that are most personal and intimate, through the narrow prism of utility.

So they work instead of play. They work in sweatshops, at construction sites, on fishing boats, and in stone quarries. They are street vendors and house girls; they shine shoes and run errands. They tend sheep, plant crops, haul water, and make bricks. In certain industries, such as mining, their small size is their chief asset, enabling them to maneuver in very small places where no adult would fit. Children are also cheaper to hire than adults. In many countries of our world children can be found doing jobs adults have shunned because the work is menial, or onerous, or dirty. Child laborers are unaccustomed to many of life's simplest pleasures: participating in sports, idling away a summer afternoon by a pool or at a picnic, playing card and board games, visiting an amusement park, inventing make-believe activities with friends. Instead, the present moment all but consumes them in an endless game of survival.

When children exist in a survival mode from the very beginning of their lives, they are denied the opportunity to learn some of the deeper and more elusive lessons of life. When will these young persons come to feel the zest, beauty, and joy of just living? What will feed their imaginations and deepen their curiosity about themselves and the community to which they belong? How will they come to know and experience the rejuvenating power of leisure? What experiences will draw them to build trusting relationships and deep attachments to others based on what love can offer instead of what is useful and necessary at a particular moment in time?

OUR WORLD'S ENSLAVED CHILDREN

In the north African country of Mauritania, other young people are engaged in the very same enterprise of selling water as Carlos and Antonia in El Salvador. Less than half the households in the capital city of Nouakchott have access to running water. As a result, three hundred thousand people in this city daily rely on the labor of those who earn their living by hauling water to homes, businesses, and construction sites. The profit margin here is relatively the same as it is for Carlos and Antonia, about four dollars a day. The crucial difference is that these young people in Mauritania are slaves and all the profits they make go to their master at the end of each day.

Of all the countries in the world, Mauritania has the largest proportion of its population living in slavery. While slavery has been officially abolished in this police state since 1980, legal freedom has yet to result in actual freedom for hundreds of thousands of enslaved people. The country goes to great lengths to hide its slave practices from foreign visitors. Indeed, Mauritania's repressive government routinely denies visas to researchers seeking to examine its compliance with internationally recognized human rights.

For slave children in Mauritania, life goes on in much the same way as it did for their ancestors centuries ago. In return for a place to sleep and a little food, present-day slaves in Mauritania put in a workday of from fourteen to sixteen hours. The economy in this nation, a land that has made slavery a permanent part of its culture, rests squarely on the never-ending toil of its slaves, too many of whom are children.

Professor Kevin Bales of the University of Surrey in England gained entrance into Mauritania in recent years disguised as a zoologist interested in researching that nation's native hyenas and jackals. His real interest was studying and documenting the economic and social forces that have sustained a primitive, tribal form of slavery in Mauritania right into the twenty-first century.

Professor Bales has observed how children and women slaves in Mauritania are especially powerless. He tells us that their lives are often so completely controlled that their slavery is not even visible:

> In their master's household the women are passed off as domestic workers or family members . . . the Koran makes female slaves available to their masters for sex. The sexual use of slave women is a key part of their subjugation, and it is one of the rights that the slaveholders are loath to give up. For the master its importance goes well beyond pleasure. Female slaves produce more slaves, and more slaves are valuable.[1]

It is ultimately inconsequential whether the master fathers the children of his slave women or not. In Mauritania the master possesses the power to claim as his own all the children born to his slave women. He also has the power to move the children to other households, to give them away to relatives and friends, and even to sell them for profit. It is the master who decides the fate of his slaves' children, not their fathers or mothers.

The man who fathered Carlos and Antonia in El Salvador made a decision to abandon his children. Slave fathers in Mauritania generally do not face such a choice. That decision is usually made for them by the slave owner. The natural fathers are virtually powerless to claim their moral and legal rights to raise their own children and to keep their families intact, even when they desire to do so. Professor Bales describes the mind-set of a male slave:

> The result is fatalism and resignation. Denied rights over their dependents, often separated from their families, male slaves find it psychologically easier to run away. Slaveholders are not overly eager to recover escaped male slaves, since they are not wealth producers like slave women. Men who run away may find menial jobs; though free, they often end up living in worse conditions.[2]

Children whose parents are caught up in forms of slavery and debt-bondage are in particular danger, for the slave owners may actually have more influence over them than their parents do.

Most people today believe that slavery is a historical phenomenon of the past. Professor Bales, the world's leading expert on contemporary forms of slavery, offers compelling evidence to the contrary. He estimates that more than twenty-seven million individuals worldwide are enslaved today. They are people whose labor is being extracted from them by some means of force while they are held against their wills through fear or coercion.

The majority of the world's enslaved people are young, able-bodied, easy to coerce, cheap to support, and ultimately disposable when they are no longer useful or profitable to those who exploit them. A 1999 study conducted by the Federation of Women Lawyers in Uganda uncovered the presence of 522 child domestic workers in the city of Kampala alone. The children earn ten dollars or less per month. Some of them actually receive nothing at all except a place to sleep and a meager ration of food in return for their labor. Yet the obvious economic injustice is only one aspect of their abuse.

Listen to the narrative of an eleven-year-old housemaid who works in a suburb of Kampala. As she tells her story to Lydia

Mirembe, a Ugandan journalist, we can judge for ourselves what it is that that her employer is stealing: Is it just her labor, or is it her entire life?

> Where I work, they do not allow me to play with anyone. They do not allow me to go to the neighbors. They do not allow me to eat before everyone else has eaten. I cook the food and serve them, then I wait for them to finish eating. I wash their plates and that is when I get to eat. On Sunday when my boss does not work, she cooks the food. But when it is about to be ready, she sends me to fetch water, or to the market. By the time I come back they have finished eating and they have left very little for me. Sometimes I don't get to eat anything because I find the food finished. When I ask them to pay me, they say that they send my money to my mother in the village. I don't think that is so.[3]

The harsh reality of this young girl's everyday life is a sad, shocking, secret story of exploitation. We should not be surprised that she is not allowed to have contact with people outside the oppressive home environment. It is likely that the natural moral sentiments of others would make them her advocates if only they knew the truth about her daily living conditions. There is a revulsion we feel at discovering the details of precisely how the strong prey on the weak. That revulsion often becomes the first link in the chain that will join us to the one harmed. Connecting with victims, even only in our revulsion toward their oppressors, unites us with them and can eventually lead to hope and help.

This eleven-year-old girl cannot be expected to fully understand the rights that are hers or the responsibilities her employer has for her well-being. Without the chance to get some schooling, without the opportunity to have the everyday exchanges with others that we all take for granted, this child leads a life that is severely limited. The story of her life is shrouded in secrecy, but it is a story that, with few modifications, is replayed all over the world, every day. It is estimated that there are some three thousand household slaves in the city of Paris alone. Their lives are not their own. They belong solely to their employers in a contemporary form of slavery that brutalizes and controls young people.

Many child housemaids eventually come to feel betrayed by a society that, at least implicitly, tolerates their subjugation. This betrayal is far more stinging when it originates within the family. Juliet, a thirteen-year-old Ugandan girl, was placed in the custody of her aunt by her parents. While education was promised, only work was given. Juliet relates what happened to her:

> I live with my auntie. She took me from my parents in the village and said she was going to bring me to a good school in Kampala. But when we came to Kampala, she did not take me to school. Now, my auntie goes with me to the market and I help her sell food. She sells cooked food in Owino market. We get up very early in the morning and walk from home in Namuwongo to the market. We get there by 6:30 a.m. and we start preparing breakfast. We cook *katogo* and tea for the people who work in Owino. Then we start preparing lunch for them. The whole day is spent cooking. My auntie does not allow me to eat food before all her customers have eaten. The men in Owino disturb me. They are always touching my body. When I protest, they abuse me. My auntie says that it's all right for them to touch me as long as they give me the money for the food. She says that I should treat her customers well and give them everything they want. But some of them ask me to sleep with them. I feel bad. My mother always told me it was not right for men to touch me.[4]

Countless young people like Juliet are forced to grapple with a very difficult dilemma. When they receive conflicting messages from adults in their own families, they must make a choice. Their future to a large extent depends on whose voice they listen to at that moment. Juliet remembers her mother's guidance, but her aunt's daily counterclaims are becoming increasingly difficult to withstand.

EDUCATION—THE KEY THAT OPENS THE DOOR TO THE FUTURE

In James Boswell's biography *The Life of Samuel Johnson,* the author tells us of a delightful boat ride he enjoyed in the company of the legendary Dr. Johnson, one of eighteenth-century England's most renowned educators and prolific writers. Their excursion took place on a beautiful spring Sunday afternoon in 1777. They journeyed on the River Thames from London to Chelsea and, as was the custom of the day, they had hired a young boy to row for them.

In the course of their lively conversation, Boswell asked his companion: "Do you think everyone should have a liberal education, Dr. Johnson?"

Johnson answered, "No, not necessarily, not everyone could use a liberal education, not everyone could profit from a liberal education. For example, to learn Latin or Greek [which of course a liberal education included in those days], what would it profit most people? What would it profit this boy who is rowing our boat? What would it matter to him to learn Greek poetry? Could it mean anything to him to learn what the Argonauts sang as they rowed their boats?"

Then, sort of jokingly, he asked the young lad rowing the boat, "Boy, what would you give to know what the Argonauts sang as they rowed their boats?"

The reply from the boy was swift: "Sir I would give everything I have."

Boswell tells us Johnson was so pleased with this statement that he tipped the boy double.

Education increases one's life opportunities and the richness of one's understanding of the world. This anonymous boat boy in

1777 London likely had an enormous thirst to discover the truth about the mysterious world that lay beyond the confines of his immediate experience of daily ferrying people up and down the Thames. Small wonder that, when questioned about his desire to know more, his answer to Dr. Johnson was so impetuous.

Nearly a billion people entered the twenty-first century unable to read James Boswell's classic biography of Samuel Johnson or any other book, nor can they identify themselves for others by signing their own names. In a world that is scientifically and technologically advanced, how have we allowed this injustice to happen?

Exploitative child labor practices, especially in the developing nations of our world, are both a result of extreme poverty and a chief cause of its continuance. As children forego education in order to help meet the immediate demands of family survival, their poverty is assured for yet another generation. That is why there exists in our day a global, moral summons to open education's doors to the nearly 120 million school-age children who are not in school, especially young girls. A full two-thirds of those whose future is today being stunted by illiteracy and the denial of educational opportunities are female.

If the inequalities that harm the well-being of women and children are to be eradicated, it is certain that the liberating power of education will pave the way. The former minister of education in Mozambique, Graca Machel, is a teacher and has been a life-long activist for expanding educational opportunities for all children. She has been a witness to the transformative power of education in our day. Graca Machel and her husband Nelson Mandela, the former South African president and Nobel laureate, are currently leading the Global Partnership for Children. She tells us why children's education remains her most urgent concern: "I have seen how one year of school changes a child and how years of school transform that child's future. I have watched as the power of education saved families from being poor, babies from dying and young girls from lives of servitude. And I have lived long enough to see a generation of children, armed with education, lift up a nation."[5]

Whatever opens a child's mind, frees a child's will, brightens a child's imagination; whatever imparts to a child courage, hope, and insight—this is precisely what we owe our young people. Nothing less will enable a faltering humanity to recover its way. The truest indicator of the vitality of communities and nations is found in the measure of opportunities given to the youngest generation to reach their full human potential. These opportunities, by moral right, belong to every child, female and male, born into the human family.

The governments of Barbados, Botswana, Costa Rica, Malaysia, Mauritius, the state of Kerala in India, along with other governments in the developing world, now hold to a deliberate policy of strong investment in children's education. They have kept their primary schools tuition-free, assuring the least advantaged children a greater chance at enriching their lives. When children today occupy the center of a community's attention, future opportunities for social and economic progress abound for all of us.

ONE HUNDRED MILLION MISSING FEMALE MEMBERS OF THE FAMILY

Subtle yet deliberate neglect of female children is a dark part of the human story that too often goes untold. The poet Tagore is said to have once remarked that every child comes into the world with a divine message: that God is not yet tired of our world, that, indeed, our Creator delights in every one of us. If every child bears this divine message, if every female and male child is *imago Dei*, why is it that strong cultural biases can prevail over one of our most deeply held moral sentiments?

If boys and girls in every family, in every region of the earth, were given equal access to nutrition, basic health care, nurture, education, and the opportunity to grow into fully responsible adults, it is likely that our world would be quite different. It is the studied opinion of economist Professor Amartya Sen that we would have approximately one hundred million more females alive today. In what regions of our world is the male-female ratio most imbalanced?

Demographers have long been aware that there are fewer women than men in some of the world's poorest countries; this contrasts with most of the developed world, in which there are more women than men. In North America, Japan, and Europe, for instance, the life span of women is longer than that of men. It is important to note that in these societies women are generally better educated, their access to health care is protected by law, and their social standing in the community is more valued than that of their sisters in India and China.

In India (especially the states of northern India), China, Bangladesh, Pakistan, North Africa, and West Asia there exists today a problem of basic inequality of extraordinary proportions. In these lands, for a variety of reasons, the potential capacities of females are thwarted early on in childhood. The chief culprit seems to be impersonal, societal forces that give preference to male children in many areas including, but not limited to, nutrition, health care, and, most especially, education.

Numerous studies sponsored by the United Nations, the World Bank, the World Health Organization, and a vast array of other nongovernmental organizations point conclusively to the fact that female education is the most effective force in our day for countering poverty, childhood diseases, and malnutrition. An educated mother, sharing herself and her acquired knowledge with her offspring, is a primary asset in any society, and most needed today in the poorest nations of our world.

The effects of societal forces that give preference to male children are particularly evident in China, where the female shortage has seen a dramatic worsening at the end of the twentieth century. In the year 2000, nine hundred thousand fewer female births were recorded than should have been; this assessment is based on statistical estimates as well as the actual male birth rate. In 1990 the shortfall was considerably less, approximately half that number. Why is there such a great disparity?

Demographers at the Chinese Academy of Social Sciences in Beijing point to a variety of reasons, including gender-based abortions, giving up unwanted daughters for adoption without registering their births, and the fact that rural Chinese women tend to breast-feed newborn girls for shorter periods, thus lowering their chances for survival. Demographers believe that in some rural areas of China 80 percent of children from five to ten years of age are boys.

The "one-child policy" that China has sought to implement since the reforms of 1979 has had disastrous consequences. In legislating family size, the state has, in effect, assumed a right that does not belong to it—the deeply personal, moral decision regarding how many children to have. This loss of individual moral autonomy is itself a major social loss that can not be overstated. Moreover, it points to serious problems in the future.

To ensure conformity to the one-child policy, local Chinese governmental officials have chosen to punish nonconformers by withdrawing social supports from all members of these families, thereby penalizing the children already born. The economist Amartya Sen is especially concerned about the adverse effects of the one-child policy on females. He notes: "In a country with a strong preference for male children—a characteristic shared by China with India and many other countries in Asia and north Africa—a policy of allowing only one child per family can easily be particularly detrimental for girls [and take] the form of fatal neglect of female children. This, it appears, is exactly what has happened on a fairly large scale in China."[6]

THE COST OF EMPOWERING THE NEXT GENERATION

At least six hundred million children and adolescents today belong to families struggling to survive on incomes of less than one dollar a day. How will we ever end the patterns of poverty that condemn this multitude of our sisters and brothers to a bleak future? I suspect it will necessitate not only a far greater investment in education and health care, but a determined resolve by those of us able to imagine a future filled with possibilities to be in solidarity with those who cannot.

Anyone who visits the campus of the University of Central America in San Salvador today can observe the cost that has been paid in this violent region to arm the next generation with education instead of deadly weapons. On the fateful night of November 16, 1989, six Jesuit priests, scholars at the school, were slain along with their housekeeper and her daughter. In grave irony, they were shot in the head, as if to say, "In this place in the world, the ultimate danger is to use your mind." Photographs of the bloody scene where they were brutally slaughtered are on display at the school. As I examined these photos, I had to force myself not to look away but to see clearly the sacrifice that was made that night.

These Jesuit teachers were unarmed, but they were not harmless. They were gifted and knowledgeable persons, possessing the capacity to help empower the next generation to uplift a nation from economic and political oppression. Imparting such an education has, historically, often proven to be a dangerous adventure. To those in darkness, light can be a powerful threat. For those who have been silenced, the freedom to speak the truth is frightening.

These scholars had been repeatedly urged to abandon their teaching positions at the university and flee to a safer environment outside the country. They embraced a costly solidarity instead, and signaled to the world the depth of their commitment to change the world through education. If those who ordered their execution wished to send a message by having them shot in the head, perhaps they more appropriately should have ordered that the Jesuits be shot in the heart. After all, people don't die for what they know with their minds; they die for whom they love.

EDUCATION AND THE FUTURE

The Jesuits slain in San Salvador had committed their lives to spreading the truth, to lifting up a world where young people can find happiness in developing their own personal identity. Our world's vulnerable children desire to be in school. They deserve to be in school communities that maximize their participation and encourage them to embrace their own rights and responsibilities for fashioning the future. In service of this goal, a growing number of educators share the conviction that new classroom methods need to be employed, methods that encourage active learning and the imparting of values rather than passive acceptance of facts. Far too many schools routinely fail to be *transformative*. Of the two purposes of education—to make a person fit for the world as it is, and to empower a person to be able to change it—Jesus taught that the latter is more important.

A relatively new educational movement in Latin America is proving to be highly transformative. While the framework for the Escuela Nueva model is still evolving, in its schools children's rights and democratic involvement in the school community are paramount. Teaching and learning are participatory, and creative teachers partner with parents and the wider community. At the heart of this enterprise is a belief in the vast potential that lies in empowering the next generation of leaders with a fresh and peaceful vision of our common future.

Many of the children in the Escuela Nueva movement have known nothing but conflict and violence all their lives. At school they are invited to discover their freedom to build another kind of world. They do this by establishing friendships with others different from themselves, accepting responsibility for other persons, acquiring leadership skills, and claiming responsibility for the discipline, learning, and cultural activities in their own schools.

These new schools are extremely popular with the students, as is evidenced by an attendance-and-completion rate of 93 percent, far above the regional average. Young people instinctively want to promote a culture of peace and democracy. They were the first to suffer from the lack of peace and stability in their homelands. Companioned and mentored by adults who know how to nurture their deepest aspirations, these young people will be the artisans of the new day that humanity awaits—a time in which war will be relegated to the past.

Notes

1. Kevin Bales, *Disposable People: New Slavery in the Global Economy* (Berkeley, Calif.: University of California Press, 1999), 111.

2. Ibid.

3. Quoted in Lydia Mirembe, "Children Tell Their Tale of Exploitation," in *The New Vision,* June 11, 2001, p. 24.

4. Quoted in Mirembe, "Children Tell Their Tale of Exploitation," 25.

5. Graca Machel, quoted in UNICEF, *The State of the World's Children 2001,* 6–7.

6. Amartya Sen and Jean Dreze, eds., *The Amartya Sen and Jean Dreze Omnibus: Comprising Poverty and Famines, Hunger and Public Action, and India: Economic Development and Social Opportunity* (New York: Oxford University Press, 1999), 65–66.

Fedora/Maryknoll

Street boys in Peru having a meal of hot soup.

4
To Feed a Hungry World

Juanita, Pedro, and little Maria were the joy of their young parents' lives. The children basked in the glow of their parents' affection while the mother and father saw their own future in the faces of these three God-given gifts that they had loved into life. Then one day, in the space of a few terrible moments, the children saw their world crumble under the weight of their collapsing adobe brick home.

Their mother had been home alone after a busy morning of washing clothes and other domestic chores when a powerful earthquake heaved the ground underneath her. She was buried alive in her own home as her husband and children raced futilely to rescue her.

When I met Juanita, Pedro, and Maria they were the hungriest children I had ever seen. Two catastrophic earthquakes had rocked their homeland in January and February 2001. The entire region of St. Vincente, a mountainous area of central El Salvador, had been engulfed in chaos after the earthquakes. Families were decimated, crops and homes were destroyed, every semblance of normalcy had been wiped out. Some children had lost one or both parents. Food was scarce.

Shortly after the earthquakes, I was visiting some missionaries from Cleveland who minister in El Salvador. I saw young Salvadoran families who had been spared the effects of the earthquakes preparing humanitarian outreach to families in crisis, often at enormous personal cost to themselves. I saw families who possessed very little quickly willing to give away the scarce food they had to feed their sisters and brothers who had nothing. Their generosity astounded me.

One afternoon, the father of Maria, Pedro, and Juanita sent his children down a hill to meet an arriving emergency supply truck. I was on that truck and was not prepared for what I would see. Several hundred distraught and hungry people—most of them children —were anxiously awaiting the warm meals of chicken and rice we were bringing. Yet that father remained alone on the hill. When I got out of the truck and glanced up at him, our eyes met. The look I saw on his face frightened me. It was the look of a person who really isn't sure whether he wants to live or die.

A week earlier, while out on a short midmorning walk, this man had witnessed the destruction of the tranquillity and love that had made his family life so rich. While approaching his home from a distance he could see its walls collapsing. Even before speaking to him and learning this about him, I knew that he had been devastated by the calamity that had struck his nation. It was all there—etched on his face.

I decided to stand in the food line for him, desperately wanting to do something to help, even something small. I felt embarrassed at first. Needy people looked at me and wondered why I, who look so well-fed, was in line for the food that had been brought for them. In a simple gesture of friendship, I climbed the hill and placed a plate of warm food into the young father's hands. The look he gave me in return will be forever fixed in my memory. It was a glance that said: "I realize my children and I can live if someone helps us re-gather hope."

The food that was shared then would bring more than release from the physical pain of hunger. The human solidarity expressed in this simplest of acts of giving and receiving enabled that father to reclaim hope for his entire family, especially for his children's future. He would eat to live for Juanita, Pedro, and Maria.

This is why all the great religions of our world command their adherents to feed the hungry. In the elementary act of providing food, we human beings share more than nourishment. Food being passed from our hands to another's symbolizes life flowing from ourselves to the other. That afternoon in El Salvador, a mysterious and holy energy bridged the gulf of separation between a despairing Salvadoran father and me. An exchange of food took place, but there was also a glance of recognition, a moment of human and spiritual solidarity.

Novelist and Presbyterian preacher Frederick Buechner, in his remarkable work *The Hungering Dark,* captures eloquently how one grace-filled touch can reverberate with a nearly endless force. He compares humanity to an enormous spider web:

> If you touch it anywhere, you set the whole thing trembling
> ...As we move around this world and as we act with
> kindness, perhaps, or with indifference or with hostility
> toward the people we meet, we too are setting the great
> spider web atremble. The life that I touch for good or ill
> will touch another life, and that in turn another, until who
> knows where the trembling stops or in what far place and
> time my touch will be felt.[1]

That young father touched my soul with his unspoken gratitude for my being by his side in that moment of pain. There was a wondrous reciprocity to our exchange. I sense that we both left that encounter more deeply in touch with the mysterious links that weave the human family together.

What drives the human family apart? I have come to believe that the harshest division in the human family today remains the ancient scourge of hunger. There is an exceedingly painful divide between those persons who get enough to eat and those who do not. All other differences among us pale in comparison.

Somewhere today on the Korean peninsula a young father will not eat so that his children might live another day on the very meager rations that he has denied himself. Somewhere in the southern region of the Sudan a mother, who long ago has forgotten herself, will have the seemingly impossible task of deciding which of her children will eat today and which will not. Denied "food security" and their place at the table of life, 790 million of our hungry sisters and brothers, the majority of them children, wait for fresh hope. Perhaps they wait for someone to touch the human spider web with compassion. Perhaps they pray that God will, at long last, endow some of us with the requisite resources and skills to move humanity out of hunger and into a new era of freedom from want.

The promise of a more humane, hunger-free world is not utopian—it is already within humanity's grasp. In the early 1970s, 35 percent of the world's people went to sleep hungry each night. That figure has been cut by half, even while the global population has increased. The world's food production has more than doubled in the last forty years. Some may choose to point to the obvious advancements in fertilizers and pesticides, the arrival of scientific farming, and new, more highly successful forms of irrigation as the chief causes of this good news. While human ingenuity has been important, no answer is complete without recognition of the role human solidarity has played in reducing hunger.

The impact of human solidarity cannot be measured or demonstrably proven—but its presence is real and effectual. As we discover new and creative ways of perceiving and more rigorously protecting the invisible ties that bind us to each other, the last day of hunger on the earth draws closer. But it all begins with that simple yet awesome recognition of what we mean to each other.

Lessons of Childhood That Last a Lifetime

Ideals rooted in human solidarity can be seen far more clearly in a person's life than in all the theories proposed to describe them. The life of the Indian economist and philosopher Amartya Sen captures in many remarkable ways our striving for a world set free from hunger and deprivation. Amartya Sen's first name, bestowed on him personally by Rabindranath Tagore, the Nobel Prize–winning Bengali poet, means "one who deserves immortality." The hungry children of the earth may one day be the first to rise up to affirm the suitability of that name.

In 1943 Amartya Sen was a child, barely nine years old, when one of the worst famines of the twentieth century broke out in his homeland of Bengal in the western region of India. Between two and three million people died. Amartya saw some of his compatriots die of hunger-related causes. It was an image that would never leave him. Later in life, as he worked with some of our world's most distinguished economists while teaching at Oxford, Harvard, and Cambridge universities, he constantly discussed how those deaths might have been prevented.

Many economists view their academic discipline as a value-free social science. Amartya Sen sees the chief and highest interest of economics as expanding human capabilities and freedoms and contributing to the well-being of all. Sen has shown himself a master at persuasively presenting a plea that the quality of our lives should be measured not by our wealth but by our freedoms and by our solidarity, especially with society's weakest members.

As a child of well-to-do parents in the early 1940s, Amartya Sen found it puzzling that none of his classmates, relatives, or friends were directly affected by the devastating famine. In fact, even those in the lower middle class were relatively protected from the onslaught of hunger. At a very young age Amartya could sense that it was those much further down the economic ladder, especially the landless rural laborers, who were most vulnerable and who were the ones dying.

Amartya Sen was also a witness to compassion amidst this horror in his childhood. He remembers seeing members of his family giving small tin cups of rice to hollow-eyed refugees. He has vivid memories of the sense of solidarity that inspired his family and others to reach out to those desperately seeking to stave off their hunger. They saw the ethical appeal in the face of the vulnerable other and Sen was instructed by the sheer force of their example to do the same.

No one could have predicted then that this nine-year-old child who just wanted to help feed the hungry strangers at his doorstep would one day revolutionize the way governments around the globe respond to the threat of famine. It was that initial encounter with hunger and the desire it evoked within his family to respond with care that energized Amartya Sen's determination to bridge the vast chasm in our world that separates those who must worry daily about whether they will get enough to eat from those gifted with a lifetime of food security.

An incident witnessed by Sen as a young child deepened his determination to bridge that chasm. A Muslim day laborer named Kader Mia worked every day in the predominantly Hindu neighborhood of Dhaka where the Sen family lived. Numerous clashes had occurred between Muslims and Hindus during the previous weeks, and Kader Mia's wife had urged him not to go to work that day in the Hindu-controlled region of the city. She sensed it was just too dangerous for him. He felt compelled to go, however, because his children had nothing to eat and needed him to work. Kader Mia was knifed in the back by some thugs that day on the street near the Sen home. Bleeding profusely, he came running toward Amartya. Amartya Sen's father took him to the hospital where he later died of his wounds.

Childhood memories of the Bengal famine of 1943 and the attack on Kader Mia left an indelible impression on the young Amartya Sen. As a child, he was gifted with a core conviction that human beings must not abandon each other when times turn rough, when some have little or perhaps even nothing. Sen grew up knowing well that compassion must be allied with knowledge and understanding if it is to succeed in bringing new promise to the lives of the dispossessed.

Wars, ethnic fighting, and exorbitant military spending are the natural enemies of us all, but most especially of humanity's hungry children. We all want peace, fairness, and enough to eat, yet the poorest children of impoverished countries often remain trapped in a cycle of war, ethnic violence, drought, and starvation.

This suffering is perhaps nowhere more pronounced than in Afghanistan. The Afghan people are no strangers to misery. Their nation, which in the year 2000 suffered its worst drought in over thirty years, does not have the history of social solidarity and good governance that has saved other nations from famine during times of drought. In this militaristic nation of twenty-seven million people, it is clearly the children who have suffered most from the ongoing civil war, closed borders, bombed roads, millions of hidden landmines, and international isolation. Sadly, Afghanistan exemplifies more dramatically than any other place on earth how violence and hunger are connected. The American-led war on terrorism that was waged in great part in Afghanistan disclosed for all the world the horrific plight of the children of this land.

Throughout his academic career and extensive research projects, Amartya Sen has sought to suggest creative ways to help break the chains of economic misery that deny elementary freedoms to vast numbers of people. These chains allow hunger, lack of basic health care, illiteracy, and other forms of severe deprivation and inequality to continue unabated despite unprecedented increases in global wealth.

The seeds of Amartya Sen's economic and social science theories were planted in childhood and help explain why he is hardly a typical economist. Other leading economists are known for having devised dubious forms of wealth creation or for formulating speculative economic theories. Amartya Sen is known for having drawn the world's attention to the 1.5 billion members of the human family—many of them malnourished children—who subsist on less than two dollars a day.

On October 14, 1998, the Royal Swedish Academy announced that Amartya Sen had been chosen to receive the Nobel Prize in economics. Professor Sen, the master of Trinity College, Cambridge University, has given the world a lifetime of careful scholarship which, according to the Royal Swedish Academy, "has restored an ethical dimension to the discussion of vital economic problems."

When he received this coveted honor, Amartya Sen explained why his research had drawn him to examine the economic and social forces that hamper the well-being and freedom of our world's dispossessed members. He stated succinctly: "I have never forgotten the human face of hunger." With diligence and acumen he has set about proposing ways in which even impoverished societies can improve the well-being of their least advantaged members.

WITH ARMS STRETCHED WIDE OPEN

The story is told of a man on a hunting expedition in Africa who left his camp early one Sunday morning to hike deep into the jungle. When he heard the sound of wild birds, his spirits soared. He was an expert marksman. After shooting two of the birds, he proudly tied the trophies to his belt and began his long trek back to camp.

While he was on his way, he suddenly sensed danger. He could see no one. Still, he felt certain that he was being followed. Keeping his finger on the trigger of his rifle, he moved slowly, carefully looking in every direction.

His panic turned into relief when he discovered it was a teenager who had been following him at a distance. The boy was naked and very thin. He was obviously starving. The hunter turned to him and decided at that moment to gift his hungry companion with his catch. Untying the dead birds from his belt, the man placed them on the ground, all the while gesturing to the boy that he could have them. The boy raced up to the birds and then stopped. Inexplicably, he did not pick them up. The hunter again tried to communicate to the youngster that he could have the birds. The boy looked with longing at them, but refused to take them. He then raised his eyes to the hunter and, with arms stretched wide open, silently invited the man to place the birds in his arms. Despite overwhelming fear and deep hunger, the boy refused to take them on his own. He waited until the gift was given. Then he received it with sheer joy.

Children, by God's gracious design, are skilled in the art of joyful reception. They delight in receiving the gifts of food, affection, and nurture from their parents. Their spontaneous embrace of these gifts is one of the rich blessings the human family holds close to its heart. When these gifts are withheld, unspeakable pain ensues—for children and parents alike.

In famine-stricken northern Nicaragua, Aura Herrara possesses only one driving ambition. She wants to give the blessings of food and nurture to her four children. She has often heard her

children plead: "Mama, can we get some food?" She forces herself to answer honestly and in a reassuring tone of voice, "You
have to be strong because there is nothing I can do." These are the
most devastating words a parent can be forced to speak to a son or
daughter. Whenever she hears her children cry from hunger, Aura
is near to despair. Still, with enduring faith she tells me: "I have
hope and faith that God will give us our daily bread. I have faith
in him and give thanks even when the bread doesn't come daily."

There exists in our day a moral imperative to provide food security to Aura's four children and to every child in every corner of
the world. No endeavor is worthier of encouragement than this
one. If we are to prevail over the violence of hunger, we must create a greater sense of solidarity, for the hope that bolsters Aura's
spirit comes in the form of bread—bread supplied to her by others
who know they are connected to her family by the invisible links
that tie the human family together.

MAKING A PERSONAL COMMITMENT TO HUMANITY'S HUNGRY CHILDREN

Every day, somewhere on this earth, twenty-four thousand people
—the vast majority of them children—die from hunger. A recent
report by the United Nations warns that a hunger crisis currently
threatens 8.6 million people in Central America alone. Earthquakes, hurricanes, and plummeting coffee prices have sent this region of the world into deep turmoil; its children are at great risk of
malnutrition and hunger-related illnesses. The situation in Africa is
even more precarious. It's easy for individuals to feel overwhelmed
and helpless in the face of the sheer magnitude of this problem.

Each day, I click on the website www.hungersite.com and an
image mapping the entire globe appears on my computer screen.
Every three seconds a nation in that picture darkens, indicating a
death by hunger. India darkens more frequently than any other
country, but Madagascar, Russia, Iraq, Mexico, North Korea,
Bangladesh, Afghanistan, Sudan, and a score of other places in
our hungry world also darken frequently. Sometimes I sit at my

computer for long periods of time and just watch as areas of the world map grow dim. I am filled with sadness and bewildering thoughts when I try to grasp the depth of the world's disparities. How is it that in the United States today we are seeing more and more food-eating contests in which obscene amounts of food are consumed for sport and the nation suffers from an epidemic of childhood obesity? Are we so far removed from our hungry sisters and brothers that we cannot hear their cry?

During my time in East Central Africa I would occasionally go with my host on long walks down untraveled, remote roads. One summer afternoon we walked for miles and encountered only two other travelers, a young mother with her small child strapped to her back. The child was sick with malaria and the mother was returning from a fifteen-mile journey on foot to the nearest hospital. She had enough money for the medicine for her child but absolutely nothing else. I asked her if it would be all right for my friend and I to provide the bus fare for them to get home quickly, since the child appeared to be quite ill. She answered by kneeling in the dirt and kissing each of my fingers.

Within two minutes, a bus going in the direction of her village came roaring down this remote road. But the young mother did not flag down the bus. I asked my host what he supposed was the reason. His conjecture was that our gift to her provided something far more essential than transport. It was seen by her as food security for her children. At a desperate time, in a future moment when there would be no other way to provide food or medicine, this seemingly small gift would become the blessing holding her family together. She would walk home in joy and in gratitude, carrying her sick child, knowing that she now possessed a measure of security to protect her family.

This young mother sowed the seeds of gratitude in my life. I have known a lifetime of food security. I have never even once wondered how the next meal might be provided. Since having met her, I am more conscious of this privilege and profoundly grateful for this previously unrecognized gift.

Often I revisit in my memory that brief encounter. When I am sitting at my computer and a country in East Central Africa darkens, I spontaneously imagine the face of her child. I can still feel the gentle touch of that mother holding and kissing my hands. The darkness on the map before me now could represent the death of someone in her family. Her protective love for her children inspires me to search out new ways to be in solidarity with those whose future depends entirely on their staying connected with other members in the human family who know of their plight and who care.

There is a specific, hopeful purpose that lures me and more than 220,000 individuals from around the world to visit this website daily. It is possible to click on a button marked "give free food" and, thanks to generous corporate sponsors whose logos then appear immediately, a cup of food is donated. To date, over two hundred million cups of food have been donated to aid hungry people in over seventy-four countries.

It is the simplest of actions—a single click, a touch of your finger on the mouse—and in that moment you have joined the worldwide fight against hunger. What is equally important to me is that this action, repeated daily, connects me to the hungriest members of the human family. Millions of voiceless children on our planet sense that their very survival depends on connections such as these.

NOTE

1. Frederick Buechner, *The Hungering Dark* (New York: Seabury Press, 1969), 45–46.

Lynn A. Ischay. Used with permission.

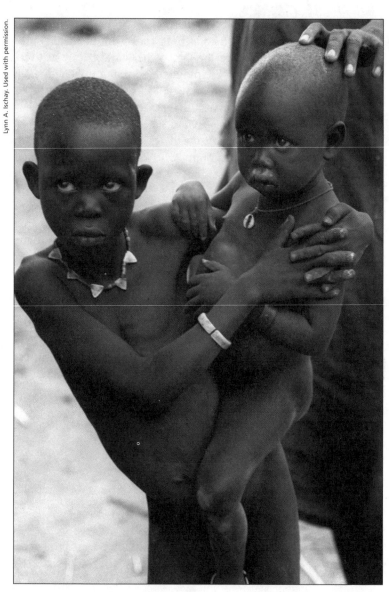

Children in a refugee camp in Tonj in South Sudan.

5
Scenes from the Refugee World

Severn Cullis-Suzuki, a twelve-year-old Canadian girl wise beyond her years, spoke at the 1992 Rio Earth Summit sponsored by the United Nations. In a captivating six-minute address she echoed the sentiments of millions of children who have, at the beginning of their lives, come to believe that there is something terribly wrong with our world. She told the leaders of nations:

> I am only a child, yet I know that if all the money spent on war was spent on ending poverty and finding environmental answers, what a wonderful place this world would be. In school you teach us not to fight with others, to work things out, to respect others, to clean up our mess, not to hurt other creatures, to share—not to be greedy. Then why do you go out and do the things you tell us not to do? You grownups say you love us, but I challenge you, please, to make your actions reflect your words.

Severn understood that love is more than an emotion: it is an abiding commitment to act on behalf of the well-being of those claimed to be loved, it means protecting their future. She was stunned when she received a standing ovation that day. Some conference participants were reduced to tears, so moved were they by the simple truth of her message. Yet, ten years later, as Severn took stock of how little had changed in our world, she lamented all the lost opportunities to fashion a violence-free world. She said: "My confidence in the people in power and in the power of an individual's voice to reach them has been deeply shaken."

At the United Nations Millennium Summit in 2000, leaders from nearly every country committed themselves and their governments to a series of ambitious and specific targets to advance humanity's common aspirations. They declared their intention to work together to halve, by the year 2015, the proportion of the world's population suffering from hunger and a lack of safe drinking water. Those leaders knew then precisely what it would take to succeed. The key factor contributing most directly to meeting this goal is peace. Severn is today most concerned about the short-sighted way in which some leaders look at the future, the way in which they fail to fathom fully what peace-making can accomplish for us all.

If the international community can achieve genuine advances in conflict prevention and post-conflict management, then this ambitious goal set at the Millennium Summit is realistic, not just idealistic and naive. Nothing destroys humanity's hopes for a hunger-free world more insidiously than armed conflict and its aftermath.

At the end of a conflict, those persons forced to flee the violence often find few if any opportunities to rebuild their lives. Violence leaves refugees a horrific legacy—the companionship of twenty-two million sisters and brothers from around the globe who have also fled their homelands in terror. There are likely an equal or greater number of internally displaced persons who, while not having left their homelands, have been forced to flee their homes and local communities for safety. The United Nations estimates that violence keeps a staggering forty-five million persons hostage to a servile way of life as refugees, either inside or outside their homeland.

In the summer of 2001 there were two million internally displaced persons in the Democratic Republic of Congo alone. Widespread hunger, a consequence of the war in this nation, affected an estimated one-third of the total population. In the capital city of Kinshasa, reports indicated that large numbers of people ate only once every two or three days.

Indelibly etched in my memory are scenes from my first visit to a refugee camp. There were people everywhere, a seething mass of humanity no matter where I looked. This was my overwhelming impression upon first setting foot in a Sudanese refugee camp in northern Uganda one afternoon in July 2001. I had read about the overcrowded conditions, but to actually see and feel them was something for which no amount of reading could have prepared me.

In fact, I had not even expected to visit a refugee camp that day. I had been traveling north from Kampala to Gulu with Father Patrick, an affable Welshman who had immigrated to Uganda thirty years earlier. Joining us were Sister Rosemary, a member of the Sacred Heart Congregation, and Alice, a pharmacist who had loaded down our vehicle with supplies for her store in Gulu. As we made our way along the four-and-a-half-hour journey north we talked, enjoyed roadside snacks, and prayed the rosary together. I was in the back seat with Alice, yet I could hardly see her. We were separated by a huge pile of boxes of condoms for the pharmacy. I thought it at least slightly ironic to be praying the rosary in the midst of all those condoms.

Sister Rosemary's provincial superior was working at a refugee camp located along our route and Rosemary asked if we could stop to pay her a visit. We all agreed to her suggestion, yet I felt somewhat apprehensive. Ten years earlier, while I was on a skiing holiday in Europe, one of my companions saw a road sign indicating that the Dachau concentration camp was nearby. He suggested that we drive over and take a tour of this infamous place. As we walked through the entrance gate at Dachau, I had the most overwhelming sense of the presence of evil I have ever known. Something horrible, something inhuman had happened in this place and I could sense it. Now, within moments of learning that we would soon be entering a refugee camp, I began to grow anxious. What would this be like?

The natural ties that bind people in the same locality include a shared language, customs, and history. In this refugee camp there were thousands of people from the Sudan whose ties to each other had been forged in a very different way. Life's brutality had brought them together. These families had been forced to flee from their homes to escape the deadly violence in the Sudan. In all my personal experience, home is where we flee to, not from, when the pressures of life mount.

As I entered the camp, many emotions welled up inside me: pity, compassion, anger at the persons and forces that had conspired to create this mess. I was also conscious of the temptation, to be avoided at all costs, of defining the people here entirely by their suffering. To do so would require ignoring the smiles I saw on the faces of the children at play, pretending I didn't see people caring for others' needs before their own.

I felt like a spectator. My stay was brief and my contact with the refugees was limited. Everyone in this camp lacked privacy. There was simply no place to turn for personal space. It struck me that, while everyone around me would sleep that night in these exceedingly cramped conditions, I would be sleeping in a private room in the archbishop's residence in Gulu. Instead of feeling relieved, I was racked with guilt. It was a feeling that would only intensify as we drove out of the camp while throngs of people took note of our departure. I felt like a voyeur.

During that short visit there was nothing I could have done to directly relieve even one single burden of the people there. I had become an eye-witness to their misery, but I had not acted in solidarity with them in any noticeable way. I would later come to wonder if I had been truly moved by their suffering. Had I simply allowed it to remain a "remote suffering," the exclusive possession of someone else? What kind of bond exists between these people and myself?

In the days that followed, I frequently returned to these questions. They seemed inescapable. I was convinced that my engagement with the people in the refugee camp had been incomplete. There had to be something more. Even if I never returned there or met another refugee, this could not be the end of the experience.

In his book *Distant Suffering,* Luc Boltanski suggests what that "something more" might be: "The spectator must not only be faced with unfortunates and see them from outside to be moved by their suffering, at the same time he must also return to himself, go inward, and allow himself to hear what his heart tells him."[1] I had avoided the full journey inward. These people from the Sudan had shocked me. I was jolted out of my complacency through this encounter. Its raw experience had somehow made me more aware of my own vulnerability.

"Love the sojourner [the stranger, the resident alien], for you were sojourners in the land of Egypt" (Deuteronomy 10:19). There is a commonality in human experience that cannot be denied. I began to reflect on the possibility that I wasn't all that different from these people. After all, every human life has deep and unmet desires. I had focused only on how dissimilar my experiences were from theirs, avoiding the more personal and painful reality of how we were alike. Perhaps some of the uneasiness and anxiety I experienced at the camp stemmed from the fact that the refugees reminded me of the frailty of all life. In them I could also catch a glimpse of my own hungers, my own mortality. We are all sojourners on the earth. That is why we need each other so much —to find our way home.

Surprisingly, in the midst of the grave deprivation of this refugee camp, what evoked the strongest reaction in me was something wonderful. It was the way in which food was handled in this place. Food had an almost sacred quality and was treated with reverence. Those who held food in their hands—whether to eat or to sell—gave the impression that they knew they possessed something very valuable. They were visibly grateful. In my own days ahead, when food is shared in joy, I will remember the reverence I saw in their company.

During my short stay in the refugee camp I came to a new understanding of how sharing food is intricately linked to both survival and ritual. We embrace one another with what is ours that we might live to celebrate what Providence has given to us!

The Protected Villages of the Internally Displaced

In the summer of 2001, in the region of northern Uganda known as Acholiland, 460,000 people were living in "protected villages," camps for internally displaced persons. This number represents nearly half the population of the region. They are there because the government of Uganda cannot secure their safety from the rebels while they are in their own homes. They have been forced to flee to these crowded camps for their survival, but the personal cost is overwhelming. Given the enormous human suffering involved in such a massive relocation of people, it is not surprising that it is the children who first fall victim.

I visited one of the protected villages on a very hot day in July 2001. One of the most unnerving sights was the scores of unattended children everywhere. I noticed immediately the reddish hair and swollen bellies, the most obvious signs of malnutrition.

The parents of these children work all day in the fields that surround the camp, digging to procure food. The older children tend to the younger ones. Very little formal education takes place. In one protected village, Acholibur, there are only four classrooms for 1,050 pupils. It appears that the principal lesson being taught is how to survive in one of our world's most inhospitable environments.

There is a great bitterness and frustration in the camps. People feel unable to sustain themselves and their families while living at a distance from their home environment. There, in the past, they were able to manage their own fertile land and produce abundant crops. Now mothers sadly tell of the pain caused by their prolonged daily absence from their children. Parents fear that since they cannot provide adequately for their children, these youngsters will simply be forced to try to fend for themselves, with all the predictable consequences of growing up too fast.

A number of women have been raped by rebels or by government soldiers while making their way to fetch water or firewood. But their greatest fears are for their children's health, not their own well-being. In the protected villages, malaria, diarrhea, and intestinal worms are rampant among adults and children, but have their most serious effects on the fragile bodies of the young.

The tribal leaders lament the loss of cultural traditions and moral values that once made them one of Africa's proudest tribes. The main means of transmitting the Acholi traditional culture to the younger generation is the evening family gathering around the outdoor fire. This is referred to in the Acholi language as *Wang oo*. Army regulations for the protected villages require that everyone be indoors or at least next to their huts by 7:30 in the evening. Non-compliance is punishable by a beating. Since it is impossible to hold the *Wang oo* without the fire and the chance to gather extended family, the elders fear they will be unable to hand on to the younger generation their legacy of solid cultural values.

It is hard to overstate the negative effects on family and community life resulting from crowding large numbers of people into a very small and restricted space. People tend to become more easily annoyed, anxious, and irritable. Parents and children sleep in the same small hut with no privacy. The huts themselves are crammed together, exacerbating the tensions of overcrowding. Domestic violence is common. Many families have spent the last five years living under these stressful conditions. A revered elder recently stated: "If this situation of displacement in the camps continues for five more years, it is going to be the total destruction of the Acholi."

Many of the boys from the camps, some as young as thirteen and fourteen years old, are already seeking to join the local defense units. Their counterparts in other, safer places of the world are still enjoying playing sports and looking forward to going to high school. The boys in the camps have few prospects other than the military. They are used to surviving on so little that the prospect of earning forty thousand shillings a month (about twenty-two dollars) is highly enticing.

Girls as young as thirteen elope with soldiers. Since the soldiers are about the only ones with money, they have acquired a reputation for using it to buy sexual favors from the camp's female residents. It is not surprising that only about 15 percent of the teenagers from the protected villages are able to pass exams to continue on to secondary school.

The population of school-going girls in the camps is proportionately lower than the population of school-going boys. This is most apparent in high school, as teenage girls become ever more involved in the necessary survival activities of the camp. These activities are time-consuming and include collecting firewood and water, standing in long lines for food rations, trading small amounts of rations for non-food items, and, of course, engaging in the domestic work of cleaning and cooking. Some girls do not attend school because they are taking care of the smaller children or have become pregnant themselves. Family and community attitudes, deeply ingrained by custom and tradition, encourage the girls to view education as the prerogative of their male counterparts. One of the teachers in the camps told me: "We have cultural setbacks. In many of our African communities, when a girl gets to adolescence, she just thinks of marriage because it will bring dowry wealth to her parents. Girls lose interest [in education] because of the expectations and cultural factors they grow up with."

Rebecca, a teenage girl bursting with energy, is an exception; she finds her interest in schooling intensifying, not diminishing. She wants to become a doctor. In her classroom in one of the camps, boys outnumber girls by a large percentage. Since her mother is deceased, Rebecca is responsible for tending to the needs of her father and brothers. She is always the first one up in the morning. An hour before anyone else in the family awakes, she can be found getting firewood and fetching water from the river. She then prepares breakfast for her family and herself, cleans up afterward, and departs for school by 7:15. She is in the classroom until 1:00 in the afternoon. Between 2:00 and 3:00 she concentrates on her homework before beginning the afternoon chores of again gathering firewood and fetching water, preparing and cooking the evening meal, and cleaning up afterward. She has promised herself that the extensive time her chores demand will not keep her from her dream. In her culture, it would be unthinkable for a male to perform these household chores.

The sad irony in these camps is that the thing that is most present is a sense of absence: the absence of food, security, education, medical supplies, clothing, hopefulness about the future, adult nurture of the children, and the slightest impression that this place is home.

THE LOST BOYS OF SUDAN

Having twice been brutally expelled from their own homeland, a huge number of Sudanese boys became family to each other on their thousand-mile trek in a desperate search for a new place to call home. They fought off lions and hyenas, the bullets of hostile governments, and the deadly heat of the Sahara, possessing nothing for protection except the brotherhood they had forged with each other. To stay alive, they were forced to leave behind everyone they loved. They had to sacrifice their cherished way of life in the Dinka culture of southern Sudan in exchange for a very uncertain future.

An Islamic fundamentalist regime in control of Sudan's capital, Khartoum, had carried on an unrelenting persecution of the non-Muslim Sudanese, especially the Christians, in the southern regions of the country. Thousands of young boys and adolescents escaped the deadly violence unleashed upon them by their own government by fleeing, on foot, all the way to Ethiopia. When Ethiopia erupted in civil war in 1991, they were forced back to the brutality of Sudan, only to be expelled again in 1992.

The day they were routed out of Ethiopia was a day of immense suffering. The boys, approximately twenty thousand in all, were attacked by Ethiopian soldiers who opened fire on them as they descended into the dark waters of the Gilo River. This fast-moving body of water marks the border between Sudan and Ethiopia and at certain points is nearly half a mile wide. Most of the young boys had never swum before. There was no escape route except by way of the place they feared the most—the river that could become their grave. It is estimated that as many as three thousand young people perished on that single day in the waters of the Gilo. Most died by drowning, while others were eaten by crocodiles or killed by the thousands of bullets flying in every direction. It was an unimaginably horrific scene as the waters of the Gilo River turned crimson with the blood of children.

Martin Dek was barely fourteen years old when he found himself forced to cross the river or die. Some of his friends were good swimmers. At a point where the river is narrow, they tied ropes to the trees and swam ahead to secure the other ends of the ropes to trees on the opposite shore. Martin and his friends, who couldn't swim, clung to these ropes as they struggled to get from one side of the river to the other. They were barely able to keep their heads above the water in a terrifying passage that was, quite literally, from death to life.

There was utter mayhem when the boys reached the Sudanese side of the river. In the commotion, one of Martin's companions, a young boy named Daniel Peter, was pushed off a twenty-foot cliff. He landed on his face and smashed out eight of his teeth. His survival instincts took over and, despite his incredible pain, he rushed forward into the crowd and made his escape.

The boys eventually reached a region in northern Kenya where they were settled in a United Nations refugee camp at Kakuma. The Sudanese government did not want them ever to return, assuming they would be hostile toward a government they believed had sought the destruction of their families, their tribe, their Christian faith, and themselves. At Kakuma these youngsters clung to each other in the hope of retaining their identity and the values of their community.

Over the past twenty years the civil war in Sudan has claimed the lives of more than 2 million Sudanese and sent another 4.2 million people into exile. Of the 75,000 refugees crowded into the sprawling, ten-mile wide camp at Kakuma, over 70 percent are from Sudan. Others in the camp have fled from the violence in Somalia, Burundi, Rwanda, and the Democratic Republic of Congo. Over half of the population at the camp is under eighteen years of age. There are many more men and boys in the camp than women and girls. Thousands of these boys arrived at the camp as unaccompanied minors, some orphaned by the civil strife and others unable to return to their families.

What is daily life like in Kakuma? At a time when their young bodies and spirits are meant to be growing strong, these young people are ravaged by hunger as they try to survive in the camp. The UN's World Food Program has been forced to place Kakuma residents on what the agency terms "half" rations. Food is distributed only twice a month in carefully measured portions that are supposed to provide one meal per day. Most residents live on sixteen hundred calories or less each day. Hunger pangs have forced a sizeable number of residents to leave the camp and go in search of stray crops or wild edibles. While residents are not permitted to leave at will, hunger drives them to take desperate measures.

Some of the young people have been living at this camp since the United Nations inaugurated Kakuma in 1992. This is where they have grown up. At Kakuma, oftentimes living on a single daily serving of corn mush, they have advanced from childhood into adolescence and on into young adulthood. Since thousands of them have been orphaned or live with little hope of ever seeing their parents again, they have been raised in a system of group care supervised by tribal elders. Martin Dek, who is no longer in the camp, told me that he had never received formal schooling until he arrived at Kakuma. He said: "We just wanted to study to help our people back home. When we arrived at Kakuma we had no power and no knowledge. When we left Kakuma we felt like we had some of both."

When Martin began his education at Kakuma, school supplies were very scarce. A book was shared by five or more students. He remembers being permitted to have a textbook in his possession for one hour a week, and he felt that was a privilege. Martin has an insatiable appetite for learning.

Until very recently, the world has taken little note of the plight of these refugee children. Sudanese religious leader Bishop Macram Max Gassis has traveled to Europe and North America to speak on behalf of the afflicted and displaced young people of

Sudan. He describes the suffering of his people as a "hidden holo-caust." As he pleads for solidarity, he fears that few in our world have any idea of what has happened in Sudan since the war began in 1983. His message: "Come and see us, come and touch us, come and put your hands around us, and caress us! Because love is a virtue of the strong and courageous. One who is a coward will never be able to love."

While few people from North America or Europe have ac-cepted his invitation to enter the war zone, some governments have begun to realize the severity of the political instability, violence, and religious persecution in Sudan. Certain governments have opened their borders to allow a number of Sudanese refugees to find new and permanent homes within their countries. Between November 2000 and September 2001, approximately thirty-eight hundred Sudanese children and young adults, predominantly boys and young men, were resettled in the United States. They have begun the adventure of discovering a strange, new world some eight thousand miles away from their homeland. They are grateful to have each other as daily life becomes ever more complicated.

For many of the young Sudanese refugees flown out from Africa to North America, the future seemed as unknowable as the unusual food they were served in flight. Many of them refused to eat. Some resisted the strange-looking, pre-packaged dinners served to them because they feared they would be charged money and knew they could not afford to pay. Others simply had no ap-petite for something they had never seen before. One of the boys, who was extremely hungry, looked around the plane and observed all the other people enjoying their meal. He reasoned, "These other people are all human. They can eat this food. I am human too. I will eat it." He did, and his willingness to dare to stretch the boundaries of his life would continue to be tested each day in his strange, fascinating new life in the Midwest region of the United States.

On the day of the massacre at the Gilo River, it was only the most resilient boys, the luckiest and the strongest ones, who made it to safety. They were the ones who had exhibited the strongest

survival instincts on their thousand-mile trek. One young Sudanese, newly arrived in the United States, told me that in the Sahara, as they marched in the dry heat, he saved his own urine. He
had predicted there would come a time on their march when there
would be nothing else to drink. Such a time did come, and many
of his companions died of thirst. This adolescent, like thousands
of others, did whatever had to be done to stay alive.

Some of the boys, to honor their lost brothers, took on the
names of those who did not survive the journey to a new homeland. The youths who perished are loved and remembered this way.

The survival instincts of those who lived were not only for
themselves, but also for their community. These young men, now
in their early and mid-twenties, routinely send money back to
Kakuma. They earn their living as janitors, bellhops, and factory
workers. Some work two full-time jobs at minimum wage in order
to provide help for family and friends in their homeland in East
Central Africa. They have little by American standards, but they
know that those whom they love at Kakuma possess nothing at all.

After all they have been through together, the hearts of these
boys remain amazingly in the right place. It is as if they have come
to a profound understanding: there is no future for them if they are
not in solidarity with their loved ones back home. This, they believe, is the only way to be true to themselves.

They tell me that they have always sensed that God would
bring them to a safe place where they could rebuild their lives and
remain in solidarity with their relatives and friends. They have
never felt like "lost boys," because they have always had a strong
sense that they belong to God and to each other. Meanwhile, they
dream of the moment of reunion when they can again see, hear,
and touch their family members.

For Christmas 2002, I invited Daniel Peter, the boy whose
teeth had been knocked out at the Gilo River, to visit my family in
Fairview Park, Ohio. It was just one week after he had had the
wondrous opportunity to speak with his mother, Yar, for the first
time since 1987. The last time they had spoken was on Daniel's
final day with his family in Sudan, the day on which he had set

out alone into an unknown future. He had been barely seven years old then. Forced to flee the terror in his homeland, he lost his childhood that day. His mother remembers vividly the morning of his departure and the heartbreak that engulfed her as she realized that she was unable to protect her own small son.

Yar eventually fled from Sudan into Uganda in the hope of learning the whereabouts of her son. Now, fifteen years later, they finally connected. Their voices met through the same medium all of us use to reach out to loved ones: the telephone. In the initial moments of the phone conversation, it mattered little what she was saying—Daniel thrilled to the very sound of her voice.

The story was different for Daniel's mother. At first she was incredulous, finding it hard to believe that she was truly speaking to her own son. Once Daniel had convinced his mother of his identity, he listened for the next ninety minutes with utter rapture to her every word. What was her maternal advice in that memorable conversation? "Study. You must continue to study. Education is the only route for our people to secure a promising future. Work and save money so you can help the young ones here to get an education too. Your younger brother whom you have never met needs you desperately."

The odyssey of the "lost boys of Sudan" is a gripping tale of survival. Indeed, many people in North America and Europe have become quite familiar with their ordeals. The "lost boys," after enduring biblical-like wanderings in the Sahara, have become living icons of African survival. All their many adjustments to astoundingly new life-situations are now well chronicled and celebrated. Indeed, their struggles have become the stuff of African legend.

These young men, who had never been in a moving vehicle, now routinely operate computers, elevators, washing machines, DVD players, and all sorts of electronic gadgets every day. I recall the time when my companions offered a ride in our jeep to young people in East Central Africa who had never been aboard a moving vehicle. I remember having to open and close the door for them; they had no idea of how to get into a car. A more profound change in living situations is hard to imagine.

THE LOST GIRLS OF SUDAN

The story of the "lost girls of Sudan" is far less known. They were fewer in number, yet several thousand, ranging in age from eight to fifteen, and they experienced a journey similar to that of the boys. They faced the same lions and crocodiles, were injured in the same way, and knew the same hunger pains and the same despair that accompanies the feeling of being forever lost. Yet not many of them have been resettled in other countries, largely because these young girls were not able to maintain their group identity as did their male counterparts. By remaining an identifiable group, the "lost boys" caught the attention of resettlement countries. Many of the young girls, in contrast, have been absorbed into foster homes, or given in marriage by their adoptive parents for a bride-price. Some adoptive parents have been offered dowries as high as fifty cattle by suitors seeking one of these girls for marriage.

All the young girls at Kakuma engage in domestic chores. Much of their day is consumed by servile labor. The males in their society, by cultural tradition, never engage in such tasks as cooking and cleaning. These tasks, along with collecting firewood and hauling water, are reserved for the girls. At one point some very hungry young men at Kakuma were offered dry rations. Despite their intense hunger, they refused to prepare the food, insisting instead on waiting until some girls could be found to prepare it.

The chance for education, a sliver of hope in this dusty camp, is virtually lost when a refugee girl becomes pregnant. All her attention needs to be focused on her child if that child is to survive. There are special schools at Kakuma for those who have dropped out of high school for this or other reasons, but attendance is low.

When I visited the apartment of one of the "lost boys" resettled in Cleveland, I saw the face of a beautiful baby on the screensaver of his computer. The young man told me that just before learning of his opportunity to begin a new life in America he had impregnated his girlfriend at Kakuma. The charming face on the computer screen was that of his one-year-old daughter.

What is to be the fate of this baby and her teenage mother? Their situation is not an isolated one. Scores of young women find themselves in the same circumstances at this and other refugee camps. When this baby was born, another teenage girl at Kakuma also gave birth to a daughter. The circumstances of that birth, however, were much sadder. The year before, a man had entered the hut of this teenage girl, stuffed her mouth with a piece of cloth, and raped her repeatedly. She tried to conceal what had happened to her. Girls in her community feel guilt and shame for such crimes against them. She felt that if she did not conceal the crime no one would ever want to marry her. When she could no longer hide her condition, her foster parents and the refugee community rejected her. Her every day was filled with fear about the future. Eventually she was taken in by an older woman of her mother's clan who opened her heart to her. Many other girls in the same desperate situation sense the presence of God saving them if only one other person in their world does not abandon them.

This young woman named her child, the baby born of the brutal attack on her, Monday Riak. In the Dinka language the word *riak* means war. On a Monday, in the middle of Sudan's intractable civil war, Monday Riak made her appearance.

Some of the girls at Kakuma are happy for the opportunity given to the boys to board a plane and fly into a future of great possibilities. Others feel that a potential marriage partner has been removed from their midst. These girls dare not dream that anything as promising as what the boys have experienced might happen to them.

THE PROMISE OF ONE DAY RETURNING HOME

As the U.S. Army entered the city of Baghdad by force in April 2003, tens of thousands of children had already fled the city with their parents in fear of losing their lives. Many of these families left behind their homes and everything they owned. The sole possession they took into their future was each other. And what did the children of Baghdad seek most in those horrific days of peril? What all children crave—protective love. They just wanted to be held safe, in the protective arms of stronger members of the family who loved them.

While every year violence and the threat of danger disrupt the lives of well over forty million people—most of them children— the human family continues to struggle to bring some promise of hope to those who have survived the violence. I have met the face of a promising future in Martin Dek. After surviving the slaughter at the Gilo River in which many of his friends drowned, Martin has committed himself to striving for the realization of their dreams for a better world. Other persecuted persons, victimized by oppressive regimes and ancient hatreds between ethnic groups, might have walked into their future with overwhelming bitterness. Martin did not.

Martin possesses a gentle spirit, which is surprising in a person who has been forced to fight throughout his childhood in order to survive. He has fought off hunger, the deadly heat of the Sahara, and the bullets of bandits and rebel groups attempting to abduct him into their ranks. And he has fought off the propensity to stay trapped in a spirit of misfortune after years of struggle against calamities a child should never have to face—much less face alone. He embodies grace in adversity.

From the moment he arrived at Kakuma Refugee Camp, young Martin seized upon every opportunity to learn and grow. Others bemoaned the fact that they had very few, if any, resources available to them to fashion their future. Martin, on the contrary, thanked God for having saved his life. While many people in our world have a "futuristic" understanding of salvation, Martin believes he has already been saved. He discerns that his life has been spared for a purpose, that God has a definite plan for him.

Martin wants to become a healer. Gifted with a determined spirit and a keen intellect, he wants to study to become a medical doctor. Recently, the International Red Cross was able to reconnect him with his mother. They spoke via a radio connection. He was in Cleveland, Ohio, in the small apartment he shares with three other young men, all Sudanese refugees. She was somewhere near the equator eight thousand miles away. It was the first time they had communicated directly in nearly two decades. She blurted out in joy, "You sound like a man now." He proudly told his mother about his dream of becoming a doctor and returning home to her and to his homeland of Sudan. She responded with a flood of tears and cries of joy.

While Martin and Daniel and several thousand other young Sudanese have been resettled in other countries, including the United States, and given hope for a better life, thousands more remain in refugee camps and orphanages around the world. Hundreds of thousands of others, still at home with their families, live in dire poverty and hunger, with little hope for the future. Martin and Daniel invite our compassion and our solidarity in bringing hope and a future to all those who remain behind.

NOTE

1. Luc Boltanski, *Distant Suffering: Morality, Media and Politics* (Cambridge, England: Cambridge University Press, 1999), 81.

6
AIDS and Preventable Disease— Our Children in Jeopardy

Crowded three to a crib in this South African children's hospital, a three-year-old girl, newly arrived at the clinic, is as sick as any child could be. In her young life she has already suffered the ravages of chronic diarrhea, severe vomiting, tuberculosis, oral thrush, malnutrition, and a host of other ailments. Her twig-size bones are so frail that she is incapable of sitting erect on her own. She whimpers constantly as her nurse tries repeatedly to elicit a single smile from her vacant, staring face—all to no avail. Tears stream down her mother's face. She knows that sick babies rarely return home from this hospital.

This devoted mother stands very close to her daughter's crib, unwilling to leave her for a moment. She had nursed her baby for close to two years. Soon after being weaned from her mother's breast, the child grew incapable of keeping down solid food. At first the family blamed the food. Then, as multiple symptoms began to afflict her tiny body, other fears and suspicions mounted.

The child has been brought to this clinic, where a blood test will reveal that the child's underlying ailment is AIDS. Within a few days she will be dead, cradled in her mother's arms.

This mother, in her mid-twenties, is unable to read or write. She lives apart from her husband who returns home only twice a year from his work as a day laborer in Johannesburg. In Africa, many men are forced to migrate both within and outside their

CHS photo by Declan Walsh. Used with permission.

A woman cradles Georgina Everett, 4, at the Nyumbani Home
for orphans with AIDS in Nairobi, Kenya.

countries to find work. Such forced mobility helps to spread the AIDS virus far and wide.

Upon realizing her daughter has just died of AIDS, the mother says that she has heard of this disease, but does not know how it is transmitted. She learns from the medical personnel at the clinic that the AIDS virus can be transmitted by sexual activity with an infected partner. She also learns that it can be spread from an infected woman to her child during pregnancy, childbirth, or breast-feeding. She is mortified.

She has always been faithful to her husband. She begins to wonder if her husband's prolonged absence from her might have caused him to seek other sexual partners. She has had no prior indication that she or her husband might be carriers of the AIDS virus. After the death of her daughter, she confides to her female friends that she is terribly afraid to have any more babies who might suffer the same fate.

This grieving mother anticipates nothing but trouble if she were to confront her husband. Breaking the silence on AIDS and discussing sexual matters with her husband seem utterly impossible to her. Taking such a step could also entail a very high personal cost. Some women in her village have been beaten and thrown out into the streets, branded as whores, when they have dared to question their husbands' sexual activities.

In regions of Asia and Africa where AIDS is rapidly spreading, predominantly through heterosexual intercourse, many women still feel unable to protect themselves from potential infection as a result of unwanted or unsafe sex. Microsoft CEO Bill Gates has pledged one hundred million dollars to help raise AIDS awareness in India, a country that has a frightening potential for an AIDS explosion. While AIDS awareness is high in the large cities of Bombay, New Delhi, and Madras, many people in the rural regions of this vast and diverse nation have no understanding of the virus's power to kill or of strategies to prevent infection. In India, as in Botswana in southern Africa, AIDS is often spread by truckers who visit infected prostitutes and bring the virus home. Because of the enormous stigma accompanying sexually transmitted diseases, many people go to great lengths to hide the fact that they have been infected until the telltale symptoms appear.

In Assam, a northeastern state of India, a courageous woman named Jahnabi Goswami is fighting to bring this dreaded disease out of the dark. In 1994 she was a shy and naive seventeen-year-old when she was forced to enter into an arranged marriage. Unknown to her, the man her family had selected to be her life-long partner entered their marriage HIV-positive. He did not tell anyone, not even his wife, until just days before he died. He was only thirty-two years old at the time of his death. The following year their two-year-old daughter died, also a victim of AIDS.

Jahnabi is the first person in her region of India to publicly declare herself HIV-positive. She recently spoke out, saying: "I have decided to declare that I am a person living with HIV so that scores of others like me, living in secrecy among us, can come out in the open and help fight the menace by making people aware." Jahnabi is leading the march from fear to prevention in her corner of our world. Having personally experienced the pain of the terrible silence that surrounds all this dying, she plans to travel to the remotest regions of India to tell her story and to lecture on AIDS prevention. She has made a promise: "Until I die, I shall continue with my awareness campaign."

Since HIV/AIDS was first identified in the early 1980s, it has grown rapidly into the worst infectious disease pandemic ever to plague the human family. It has wreaked havoc on the social fabric of life for millions of families who have all but forgotten what the world's landscape looked like before the spectre of AIDS appeared. The number of children orphaned by AIDS is staggering. Approximately fourteen million youngsters have suffered the irreplaceable loss of a mother or father or, in the most tragic cases, both parents. And the disease continues to rage unchecked.

Scientists and medical practitioners tracking the spread of this unrelenting killer estimate that by the year 2010 the number of children who will have lost one or both parents to AIDS will have increased dramatically. At present, there are more than forty million adults and children living with HIV/AIDS. It is a disease that increasingly affects young people. Of the five million new infections in 2001, approximately half were among people between the ages of fifteen and twenty-four.

Because the HIV/AIDS pandemic robs our children of life's tenderest treasure, parental love, it poses a greater threat to more children than any humanitarian crisis the world has ever known. This single disease alone will kill more human beings than did smallpox or the great influenza pandemics or even the bubonic plague that ravaged Europe, Asia, and North Africa in the fourteenth and fifteenth centuries. There is simply nothing to which we can compare the intensity with which AIDS is now striking the human family.

Enormous resources, both intellectual and financial, have been expended in the last two decades to rid the world of this evil. Physicians and scientists, AIDS activists and researchers, governments and pharmaceutical companies have all had a role to play in the progress to date.

On many fronts, the dramatic progress in AIDS care and AIDS research is a story of the human family being drawn together to confront a deadly and common enemy: infectious disease. Within three years of the first diagnosis of AIDS, researchers had successfully identified the agent that causes this dreaded disease as the human immuno-deficiency virus. Soon after that, its genetic sequence was mapped. Many governments across the globe moved rapidly to render their blood supplies safe. Massive efforts were made by medical practitioners and researchers to learn how to use antibiotics in preventing the infectious complications of AIDS. This was followed by the breakthrough discovery of highly effective anti-retroviral therapies capable of dramatically improving the chances for survival for all those able to benefit from these costly drugs.

There has never been a comparable success story with any other disease. Yet the victories won in the fight against AIDS have not yet affected the majority of our sisters and brothers whose lives are held hostage to this killer virus. The poor, and the children of the poor, have little access to the plethora of weapons available to fight the war against AIDS. Unsurprisingly, the story of AIDS has become inextricably linked with poverty, both in the northern and southern hemispheres.

Everywhere in our world it is becoming increasingly difficult to disentangle the effects of poverty from those of disease. This is especially true in developing nations struggling to deal with the overwhelming crisis set in motion by the onslaught of the AIDS pandemic. There is a growing awareness that any plan aimed at addressing the AIDS crisis must go hand in hand with long-term strategies to seek to improve the overall health and well-being of the poorest members of the human family.

The anti-retroviral therapies have been proven to prolong life for many AIDS sufferers. These medicines are essential for survival, yet they are very expensive. This means that those who could benefit from them must either be able to afford them personally or be privileged to live in a nation that has chosen to help secure treatment for its disadvantaged citizens. There are not many such nations. More typical are countries like Kenya, for example, where although more than 2.1 million people were identified as carriers of HIV in 2001, only a few thousand were receiving anti-retroviral therapies.

The ethical debate will rage on about the various responsibilities of pharmaceutical companies, governments, insurers, and the international community to help provide life-saving medicines to everyone who needs them. Yet far too little attention is given to the many other essential weapons needed to fight AIDS and other preventable diseases: healthy lifestyles, good nutrition, healthcare infrastructures, universal education and literacy, and public policy that places a priority on its least advantaged members.

As farmers and teachers die across sub-Saharan Africa at a rate faster than they can be replaced, the students at one of America's most elite schools, Yale University, have launched a campaign demanding that the administration of their school act in concrete solidarity with AIDS sufferers. Yale is involved in the global fight against the spread of the AIDS pandemic because it earns about $40 million per year as the patent-holder for stavudine, a highly effective AIDS-fighting drug. The student body at Yale is urging university officials to use Yale's considerable influence to help ensure that AIDS drugs become more widely available at low cost in the poorest regions of our world.

The pharmaceutical giant Bristol-Myers Squibb has agreed to sell its AIDS medicines for one dollar per person per day to any African nation working in collaboration with key international agencies fighting the spread of the disease. While that price is a drastic reduction from the $10,000 to $15,000 per year that these drugs command in North America, it remains far more than what households in the developing world can afford. Current estimates at the World Bank indicate that 40 percent of the population in South Asia and 43 percent of the population in sub-Saharan Africa currently live on less than one dollar a day.

Global trade rules allow countries to breach patent laws in times of national emergencies. Poor countries like India and Brazil, more vigorously than other nations, have chosen to go this route. The Brazilian government has set up clinics to provide AIDS-fighting drugs to all AIDS victims free of charge. Pharmaceutical companies had predicted that people in poor regions of the world, who are often illiterate and unfamiliar with taking medicines, would not be able to master the complex regime of AIDS pills. The Brazilian government's experiment proved them wrong. With the will to live driving them, Brazilian AIDS sufferers have shown that they can manage taking their medicine as meticulously as their North American counterparts do.

NYUMBANI

Nyumbani, the first hospice for HIV-positive orphans in Kenya, is certainly one of the places in our world where the human family is being drawn together. As I arrived at the Nyumbani compound in suburban Nairobi, I knew immediately which building the children were in—their voices raised exuberantly in song filled the early morning.

The term *Nyumbani* is a Swahili word meaning "home." I soon discovered there were some seventy-five children, all HIV-positive, who are thrilled to call Nyumbani their home. They live in clusters of fifteen children to a house, each with a devoted housemother. The teenage boys share a home of their own under the watchful care of an "uncle." This family style of living allows many of the young children to exclaim "my mommy" or "my house" for the very first time. Most of the children lost both parents to AIDS while they were still infants or just toddlers, long before they had a chance to acquire specific memories of their parents or of parental affection and nurture. Many of them are now old enough to have at least some understanding that the deadly disease that robbed them of their parents now lives inside them.

There is a two-fold acceptance that characterizes these children: a spontaneous embrace of the beauty of life coupled with an acceptance of their own vulnerable condition. I had never before been in the company of children so aware of death. There had been fifty-one funerals in this house over a six-year period and the children had gathered at every one of them to pray and to sing God's praises. Some of the children who had died had been buried right in the garden at Nyumbani, their home.

Death was a constant and familiar reality in the lives of these children, yet the eucharistic celebration I attended with them was the most joyful and spirited gathering I had experienced in a long time. The children proclaimed the scriptures and dramatized the gospel. They played musical instruments and sang as if they knew that God was watching and delighting in them. At the sign of peace it seemed as if each child wanted to approach every member of the congregation with hands outstretched, obviously relishing the chance to touch so many people. Smiles and hugs were exchanged and our solidarity with each other was openly affirmed.

After communion, a small group performed a dance as a gift to Jesus. My eyes were fixed on a young girl who wore a lime green dress and appeared to be about six years old. There was visible joy in the movement of her body. Her gestures revealed the resilience of her spirit. Every one of her steps exuded vitality. It was impossible to watch her without being struck by her embrace of life.

Some of these children had experienced harassment, rejection, and even expulsion from their own families. The tragic fact is that an HIV-positive mother, simply and wrongly assuming that her newborn will not live, will abandon that child either at the maternity hospital or elsewhere. For other children, a painful discovery awaits them after the death of their parents—the awful awareness that no one wants them. Some have elderly grandparents who love them but who lack the resources and the capacity to look after them. Others have extended families who are irrationally fearful and anxious about allowing anyone, including family members, to bring HIV into their homes. Across the globe, especially in sub-Saharan Africa, communities are working valiantly to care for and take in the millions of AIDS orphans who need to be nurtured into adulthood. At Nyumbani hope is being reborn in these children through the kinds of experiences that can be had only in a loving home.

Two twelve-year-old brothers, identical twins, arrived at Nyumbani in 1994. They were parentless and had little expectation of a future. Within two weeks, one of these boys had died and his brother was in despair. The community at Nyumbani literally loved the surviving brother back into life with a four-fold approach to health care that attended to his nutritional, medical, psycho-social, and spiritual needs. He is now a twenty-one-year-old young man who, in a fragile body, has become an embodiment of hope for the younger children. The knowledge that he remains HIV-positive no longer has the power to destroy his chance to really live.

My stay at Nyumbani was filled with paradoxes: children who knew what it was like to have been scorned and pitied by others appeared willing to trust strangers with the gift of themselves. Even children who knew that death was coming radiated a vitality and joy that seemingly knew no bounds.

Among the principal caretakers of these children is a group of women religious who belong to the Congregation of the Adoration

Sisters of the Blessed Sacrament. Each sister ministering to the children at Nyumbani combines her work with extended periods of contemplation. These women spend three hours daily in the eucharistic presence, seeking to be attentive to the voice of God. Their readiness to let the Redeemer's spirit of love pass through them to the children is born in those silent hours. "Wasting time" with God is something the children enjoy as well. Especially on Sunday afternoons many of them can be found alongside the sisters in their chapel. It seems that at Nyumbani God is everybody's favorite person.

Volunteers from near and far come to Nyumbani in order to link their lives to this grace-filled community. A grandmother comes from next door every day to visit and chat with the children. Pilots for British Airways who routinely fly into Nairobi from London find their way to this home to play with the youngsters and throw parties for them. A husband and wife from Holland volunteer for six months every year; they consider Nyumbani their "second home." College students from the United States and Europe, filled with the desire to reach out in ways that make a difference, experience an unforgettable summer in the company of these children.

Nyumbani also offers a community-based outreach program that is helping to provide compassionate care to an additional three hundred orphaned, HIV-positive children in the city of Nairobi and its environs. Grandparents who take on the role of care providers for their sick grandchildren soon learn that they are not alone. The community at Nyumbani is prepared to be with them as assistance is needed. The care providers, usually the grandmothers, come to Nyumbani for the medical and nutritional training they need to care for these special children. The Nyumbani community provides medical kits, as well as ongoing support through visits by Nyumbani nurses and doctors, respite care, help in the procurement of food and medicines, and—perhaps most important—the encouraging presence of friends who share in the grandparents' desire to continue to foster life in the children God has entrusted to their care.

EMBRACING THE TIES THAT BIND

The love the children at Nyumbani evoke is the first thing I came to know about them. Like so many others, I was immediately drawn to these young girls and boys. My reaction was not one of pity, even though I knew they were afflicted with an as yet incurable disease. No, it was rather an opening out of my heart. The look they cast in my direction was an irresistible invitation to forget about myself and enter into the realm of the other, into their realm.

The most life-affirming aspect of Nyumbani is undoubtedly the grace-filled ties that bind the members of this community to each other. As children experience family bonds, many for the very first time ever in their young lives, a new reason emerges for them to grow healthy and strong. They are now surrounded by persons who have connected with them in the most personal way in which human beings can relate to one another—the way of family love. There is no substitute for the psychic security that comes from knowing that you belong to others.

The yearning to belong is by no means reserved to the children. It appeared to me that it is equally strong in the many healthy, able-bodied adults who offer themselves to this community. Their altruism, their choice to allow another's life to be as important as their own, bears its own special rewards. Above all, their self-gift links them to powerful spiritual energies that ennoble life. As they offer themselves as the gift of "family" to these children who, with good reason, may wonder if they belong to anyone, every person on earth is lifted up and the invisible ties that bind us all are strengthened.

What is the quality that distinguishes the human person as authentically human? The Christian moral tradition tells us us that the characteristic mark of being human is that, like God, we possess the capacity to give ourselves away. Daily, in moments of joy and self-surrender, the members of the Nyumbani family show the world just how human they are.

Casa Madre

In Youngstown, Ohio, at Casa Madre, a home-like gathering place for children with HIV and their families, I encountered youngsters who daily are prompted to dream about their future and to dream big. This HIV/AIDS ministry of the Ursuline Sisters is a catalyst for growth in the lives of some very sick children who otherwise might give up on life. Like their counterparts at Nyumbani in Kenya, these sisters know how to draw out the best from the young people they serve. In these children whose bodies are as frail as their spirits are strong, I saw the face of the Christ Child. At Casa Madre young people hear a lot about going to college one day and having a home of their own. They gain a newfound sense of hope about the future.

Whenever someone in the family is sick, the whole family is hurting. These children have all witnessed the devastating effects that HIV/AIDS has had upon someone they love: a mother's constant fatigue and the absence of home-cooked meals, a sister who needs to be carried when everyone else is dashing around, a brother's constant visits to the doctor, a dad who has been told that he likely has only one month to live and doesn't know how to say goodbye to his family. This is the world in which these children live.

Casa Madre helps these youngsters make sense of that world. Every child needs a place to call home—the safest place on earth. While most of the children normally do not stay overnight at Casa Madre, all of them consider it their home. It is where life comes together for them. Here the despair that has invaded their lives begins to wane and a new connectedness can be formed within a community of care.

The children of Casa Madre also live in neighborhoods and within families where violence, addiction, crime, and neglect are commonplace. When Lee, the beloved caretaker of the building at Casa Madre, was murdered on the property one night in December 2001, the sisters and adult volunteers who staff the home were absolutely horrified. The children, on the other hand, were deeply saddened, but not shocked. They are young, but they are already familiar with violence. They have witnessed deadly crimes in their own families, on their own streets.

Some of the parents of the children of Casa Madre have few self-organizing skills. One result is that such skills, as well as a healthy sense of respect for one's own body through personal hygiene, may never have been handed on from parent to child. To address this need, Sister Susan Durkin conducts a summer camp where life skills are imparted to boys and girls in a relaxed atmosphere. She makes it fun to learn together how to shop within a budget, use coupons, make a meal, wash clothes, and care for your body. She has become a stable and reassuring presence in the lives of these youngsters. They keep her phone number tucked away in their wallets or purses and they know she will always be there for them.

What is immediately noticeable at Casa Madre is that children are learning at an extremely young age how to care for each other and how to have high expectations of themselves. The older ones help in the tutoring and care of the younger ones and food preparation is done in such a way that all can participate. Children growing up in dysfunctional families where meals are rarely taken in common learn what it means to sit at a family table for supper. They gradually acquire a sense of responsibility for helping make the family meal happen. Their experiences at Casa Madre open up a whole new way of looking at their world and what they can hope for themselves.

Unlike the orphans at Nyumbani in Nairobi, these youngsters with HIV-positive status have access to life-prolonging anti-retroviral drug therapy. The Ursuline Sisters HIV/AIDS ministry operates a special clinic out of a nearby hospital to attend to the many medical needs of at-risk children. The first moment youngsters enter the clinic they are greeted with a big smile and a warm hug of welcome. There is a sense that this place is an extension of their home and that those who care for them are part of their family. The children who must come to the clinic often have a sense of ownership over the clinic space as well: it is *their* clinic. The medical team at the clinic, made up of many caring medical practitioners, becomes a stable, constant presence in their young lives.

Dr. John Venglarcik, a key member of the medical team and an infectious disease specialist, can still remember the exact day in 1981 when he learned about this killer virus. An article in the *Morbidity and Mortality Weekly Report* had caught his attention. It chronicled the medical case histories of three New York City homosexual men whose capacity to fight infections had been seriously compromised. He had a haunting sense then that this new virus would one day wreak havoc on millions of people, especially the young and the poor. Unfortunately, his dire premonition has proven true in the lives of the thousands of children he has ministered to.

A key characteristic of the treatment provided by Dr. John is his effort to connect with his patients. He tells me that his gift of warm hands and an appreciation of the awesome power of touch has been important in forging a strong bond of trust with each of these youngsters. He uses humor and playfulness to help establish good communication with them, believing that connecting to them is a crucial step in the healing process. He knows he cannot cure them, but he has healing love to share. He remarks, rather matter-of-factly, "God uses me as his hands sometimes."

Conveying to these young persons, in age-appropriate ways, the truth about their illness often takes a very special grace. The doctors and nurses know that certainly, by the onset of puberty, adolescents need to know about the nature of their illness and understand how it can be passed on to others. Dr. John's words have been met with sheer incredulity by some teens when they are told that the special circumstances of their medical condition necessitate sexual abstinence. Dr. John tells the boys: "A man must have the courage to tell his partner the truth about himself." He has discovered that this appeal to their sense of manhood has more persuasive force than anything else he could tell them.

In nearly two decades of caring for youth afflicted with HIV/AIDS Dr. John can recall only one time when he was unsuccessful with a young client. Although this teenager is still alive, he has been lost—not to death but to self-loathing. Chronic anger feeds his spirit with despairing thoughts. He has told his doctors: "I didn't do this to myself. Someone else did it to me. Since you cannot free me of this virus, nothing else really matters to me at all."

The Ursuline Sisters' HIV/AIDS ministry matters a great deal to young people living with an incurable disease. They just want a safe place where they can find guidance and hope and these are what they find at Casa Madre and its clinic. As I left after my visit with the sisters and the children, I prayed that thousands of other Casa Madre centers might spring up everywhere in our troubled world. A place—a home—like Casa Madre makes an invaluable contribution not just to children at risk of disease and in need of love and acceptance, but also to the common life of us all.

COMPASSIONATE CARE AS THE EMBODIMENT OF SOCIAL JUSTICE

Biblical justice is not as much about individual rights and duties as it is about the rightness of the human condition before God. We must ask: "In what sense can we call our world just, in what sense can we call our world God's kingdom, if eleven million young children in the human family die every year from preventable disease?"

The most credible voice for a more compassionate and just community that I have ever heard is the voice of Dr. David Abdulai. David and his wife, a nurse, operate a clinic in Ghana in western Africa. Some have begun to call Dr. David the Mother Teresa of Africa because of the pure altruism he extends to absolutely everyone in need who approaches him.

David's father was a leper. His mother had been reduced to begging to help keep their twelve children alive. Tragically, David was the only child in his family to survive to adulthood. All eleven of his brothers and sisters died in childhood of pneumonia, measles, malaria, and hunger-related illnesses.

David vividly remembers always being in need of life's essentials. The clearest and most dominant memory of his childhood is of always being hungry. It was a consuming struggle for his parents just to assure that each child had a little something to eat and drink each day. He told me that it was precisely the severe poverty of his childhood that made him want to fashion from his life a gift that would be in direct solidarity with our world's neediest people. This has become the single, driving ambition that motivates his life and medical practice. As a young man he realized that he would never know happiness until he could find and embrace a life for others.

While still very young, David converted to Christianity. Today he feeds daily on the Eucharist. His image of Christ is of a person with boundless love, rooted in mercy that is absolutely gratuitous. Jesus is the compassion of God, the one who freely lays down his life to heal and strengthen his companions. In the presence of Dr. David Abdulai I felt myself in the presence of the holy. This is a man who is remarkably like Christ.

Thomas Merton, in describing a saint, tells us that "the eyes of the saint make all beauty holy and the hands of the saint conse- crate everything they touch to the glory of God...He knows the mercy of God. He knows that his own mission on earth is to bring that mercy to all."[1] These words aptly describe the ministry of Dr. Abdulai in his clinic in Ghana. David told me, "When you express pure compassion, you actually give God to people." It has been his experience that when you offer compassionate care to others, nearly everyone expects that you must have an agenda, that you are looking for financial compensation, a favor, some fame as an exceptional person. When they eventually discover that you truly have no desire for anything in return, they are compelled to be- lieve that God sent you to them and that God's love is absolutely free and unconditional.

Dr. David Abdulai is intimately familiar with death. He has suffered, in addition to the death of his siblings, the loss of two of his own children. One succumbed to complications brought on by birth defects and the other died from encephalitis. He prays to his son and daughter in heaven. He calls them by name and asks them to intercede with God, to ask God to rain down compassion on the people who today live with little or no hope.

In his ministry with young people dying of AIDS and the complications brought on by the AIDS virus, David often encounters people who sense that nobody wants them. He has offered medical attention and love to prostitutes and those who have used prostitutes. These dejected people have been told by others that even God does not want them because of their sin. Since they are dying of an incurable disease, others are fearful of coming near them or touching them. As a result, they feel utterly rejected and believe that their fate is to die alone, unloved, and unmourned. This is the most severe form of poverty, to be completely cut off from the human family.

In Ghana, when someone dies of old age after a life filled with love, the relatives and friends put on white clothing and dance, happy that a long life has been fulfilled. But it is different for those dying young. Black mourning clothes are worn, parents wail, and there is a gnawing sense of regret within the community for the life that might have been.

David told me the story of the recent death of his mother. When she felt the end was near, she went to her son's clinic to say goodbye to her family. She spent the final three hours of her life being held, with utter tenderness, in the arms of her only surviving son. David placed her in his lap just as, when he was an infant, she had held him safely in her lap. He wrapped his arms around her frail body and simply caressed her, gently stroking her body with a loving touch. He gave her a gentle kiss for each of his brothers and sisters. David felt immense gratitude to the Creator for the privilege of being able to serve as a channel of gentleness and compassion for his own mother as she prepared to return to God. After her death in the early evening, he lay down and took the deepest sleep of his life. God filled him with a deep peace. He didn't cry or feel sad. All he knew was peace.

There is no similar peace for the millions upon millions of families whose children die young. Every year more than a million children die of malaria. Diarrhea kills an equal number of children every year through dehydration and malnutrition. Some 750,000 children die yearly from injuries, many of which could have been prevented through greater adult vigilance and care given to keeping our children's environment safe. During the past decade alone some 9 million children worldwide have been killed, injured, orphaned, or separated from their parents by war and violent conflicts.

A just, humane, and compassionate world community would never tolerate the massive indifference shown today toward the unnecessary suffering of children. Humanity's real weapons of mass destruction are hunger, preventable disease, and indifference —and these weapons of mass destruction are killing *our* children as we watch. Ultimately, there is no such thing as other people's children.

NEW IMPETUS GIVEN TO FIGHTING DISEASES THAT PLAGUE THE WORLD'S POOREST CHILDREN

In 1900 the German mathematician David Hilbert challenged fellow mathematicians to solve twenty-three of the most perplexing mathematical problems of their day. This single challenge has been attributed with sparking numerous mathematical breakthroughs as well as contributing to the development of computers. Philanthropists Bill and Melinda Gates cited Hilbert's stunning success as they launched their new challenge to the world's scientific and medical community in January 2003. The Gates Foundation offered $200 million to the quest to identify the critical causes leading to the premature deaths of millions of young people throughout the developing world and to seek cures for their illnesses.

The Gates Foundation has given $5.5 billion to various causes, with $3.1 billion earmarked for global health problems. This new initiative created an international competition for scientists to find solutions that will help rid the world of malaria, tuberculosis, nutritional deficiencies, and life-threatening diarrhea and respiratory infections in children. These are diseases that have been largely ignored because research allocations have been focused almost exclusively on diseases of the developed world. The challenge of the Gates Foundation seeks to shatter the complacency of the general public and the medical-scientific community, a complacency that has allowed a mere 10 percent of medical research to be devoted to the diseases that cause 90 percent of the health burden in our world.

At the same time that the Gates Foundation made its commitment to fight the most devastating diseases of humanity's most vulnerable, President George Bush tripled the nation's commitment to fighting the AIDS pandemic in Africa. In his 2003 State of the Union speech, the president pledged to increase to $15 billion American funding to fight AIDS in Africa. In his speech, the president quoted a South African doctor who said that, because of the lack of medicines, many hospitals simply must turn away AIDS patients with the words: "We can't help you. Go home and die." President Bush said, "In an age of miraculous medicines, no person should have to hear those words." He promised the support of the American people in working to help secure life-saving, anti-retroviral medicines for as many as possible in Africa. While some feared that the funding, which will be spread over a number of years, would not come quickly enough to address the emergency nature of the epidemic, many hailed this pledge as a new, extremely positive sign of a world awakening to the enormity of this global crisis.

EMBRACING THE ONE LAST CHANCE TO NURTURE

While studying theology at the American College in Louvain, Belgium, I twice volunteered during Christmas break to work at St. Christopher's Hospice in London, the birthplace of the modern hospice movement. This is where I first encountered memory books. Dying parents with young children were urged to preserve memories for their children. Part photo album and part diary, these books are one final act of nurture by parents who know that the time of permanent separation from their offspring is near.

The practice of making memory books has spread in the last decade from cancer patients in Britain to AIDS sufferers in Zambia, Kenya, Uganda, Tanzania, and across a continent mourning the unfathomable loss of millions of parents. Memory books are now connecting a throng of African AIDS orphans to their families. Parents, often frail and feverish in the final weeks of their battle against the ravages of AIDS, possess only one overarching ambition—to reach into their children's future. They carefully tuck into their children's memory books the hopeful expectations they will take with them to the grave, but not before first sharing them with the ones they love. All their hopes for the future center on their children.

Recently, one African mother who lives on the equator and who, like her husband before her, is dying of AIDS, wrote this to her young son: "I want you to study and to go to university and to be responsible." This mother, with indomitable hope, believes in a blessed future for her son. The greatest expectation she holds is that our world will come together in the fight against AIDS and conquer this deadly scourge. She is dying with the knowledge that her only son is HIV-positive.

What do parents want most to share with their children? The tender, nostalgic moments that have graced their lives together. They tell the tale of the day their son or daughter was born—and the joy surrounding that momentous event. They tell their child what it felt like, the burst of pride at their child's first steps. Some parents have the heroic strength to tell their children of the gratitude that enveloped their lives in the end as, growing weaker and weaker, they sensed the loving concern of their children.

One father tells of his seven-year-old daughter approaching him to ask: "Are you sick? You're not feeling well, I see it. I'm sorry. I wish I could stop the hurt." Such supportive love on the lips of the youngest among us reminds us that the compassion of God is often most clearly seen in the heart of a child. Through memory books parents are able to tell their children that they saw bravery in their eyes as they prepared themselves to meet God—and that their children's courage gave their parents strength.

Rebecca Nakabazzi, a Ugandan mother who was dying of AIDS in the spring of 2003, had a multitude of memories and a wealth of maternal advice that she wanted to give her son Julius, a shy but affectionate eleven-year-old who dotes on his mother.

First and foremost, she wanted her son to know that his face and many of his mannerisms resembled those of his father, whom Julius never really knew. He had died, also of AIDS, when Julius was only two. His mother places numerous pictures of his dad in the memory book so that Julius can see for himself. She writes on a piece of paper: "You resembled your father and at the same time me, so you are a mirror of both of us."

Rebecca Nakabazzi hopes the stories she tells in the memory book she is compiling will help fill the void in Julius's life after she is gone. She tells stories about life before the cruel disease of AIDS invaded their family. Writing them down for Julius has been a work of love, but very emotionally draining. She wishes she had begun the task months earlier, when her energy level was much higher. Nevertheless, this project has created for her one last chance to gift her son with the treasure of maternal nurture—and for this privileged opportunity she gladly spends herself.

When confronted with the question of why she appears to be exhausting herself with this project instead of resting, she replies: "When we die, a lot of memories can fade away with us. The family history can disappear. I want Julius to always remember his mother."

NOTE

1. Thomas Merton, *New Seeds of Contemplation* (New York: New Directions Books, 1961), 24–25.

A young boy who lives on the streets in Tanzania.

Wheater/Maryknoll

7
Children Denied a Place at the Table

Kampala, the vastly overcrowded capital city of Uganda, swells to nearly one and a half million people by day. The first time I set foot on its bustling streets there seemed to be children everywhere. Barely clad young people, some as young as five years old, beg daily for food on the street corners. The very way they comport themselves makes clear that their desires stretch far beyond the immediate satisfaction that will come from eating again. They crave attention. After all, they are just like all children who long to be noticed. Their eyes follow yours if you dare to look at them: They watch you watching them, and then their smiles burst forth.

I invited three of these youngsters to join my friend Peter John Opio and me for lunch. The oldest child was no more than eight years old. We sat together at a table in a fast food restaurant, but only briefly. Almost immediately the manager approached us and invited us to leave. He took my friend and me aside to explain his predicament: "I understand what you are trying to do here, but my customers are offended by your bringing these sorts of children here into our company."

In my disbelief, I was speechless. My friend, a professor of business ethics at Uganda Martyrs University, began to speak to the manager in eloquent terms: social solidarity, co-responsibility, the plight of vulnerable people. The result? We ended up eating in the street with the children. It gave me some comfort to know that, in the end, we were at least welcome to eat on the very street corner that our new friends called home.

In the restaurant the children had been very well behaved. Any parent would have been proud of them. They spoke in quiet tones. They sat with their hands folded and even their posture was perfect. Their behavior caused no disturbance whatsoever. Yet they were summarily asked to leave because the very sight of them was judged a disturbance.

Only one other time in my life had I ever been asked to leave a restaurant, and that time I had experienced the same kind of disbelief. Remarkably, when this had happened, nearly a decade before, I had been in the company of this same friend. We were both doing graduate studies at The Catholic University of Louvain in Belgium and I had asked him to join me for dinner at a place with which I was very familiar. It had great food and what I thought was an inviting atmosphere. I came to learn, however, that the sense of welcome had unspoken limits. Although I could see plenty of empty tables everywhere, I was told that there was no table for us that evening. I was confused. I had been at this very same restaurant just the week before and, while every table had been filled that night, the manager had begged my friends and me to just wait a minute, please, and he would find a table for us. Later, other friends in the city told me that this restaurant was widely known for not welcoming people of color.

At the time, my friend politely shrugged off this unwelcoming incident and we shared a marvelous meal elsewhere. While we were able to brush aside the earlier incident, it would be very different for these street children who had just been welcomed into our company and then denied a place at the table. They do not yet have a sense of their own worth. They have few inner resources to bolster them when they experience rejection. Lacking self-confidence and self-esteem, they know the awful feeling of being cast aside as nobodies.

That day in Kampala, we feared that being told they must leave the restaurant would give these children one more hurtful experience of standing apart. That is why, in their presence, my friend stood up for them and spoke to the manager on their behalf. That day they were embraced by someone with words of friendship. I suspect it may have been a long time since anyone had done this for them.

Throngs of people walk by these children every single day. Indeed, many adults are frightened of them, judging them to be thieves, a threat to their security. My friend and I knew instead that they were victims—cruelly robbed of their childhood by forces beyond their control. Parents who die or who simply can no longer raise them, physical and sexual abuse at home, alcoholism, or the breakdown of family structures can send children into the streets. In some of our world's poorest countries, children who reach the age of ten face the danger of being turned out of their homes and told to fend for themselves. Other children have been forced to go in search of love when their own homes have become devoid of the bonds that naturally hold a family together. Some are naively drawn to the streets of the big cities by false allures, expecting that freedom and fun await them. What they discover is just the opposite.

One afternoon I walked the lively streets of Kampala with a seventy-nine-year-old American Jesuit priest who has befriended the city's street children. Father Gene Hattie has spent most of his priestly ministry teaching in schools in India and Africa. Today he continues his ministry as a strong advocate for a more humane response to the crisis of homeless children. In recent years, he has been a major fundraiser for several shelters for street children opened by some of his former students. He also makes time to visit with the youngsters, both those in the shelters and those still on the street. The local police have objected to his giving attention to these children on the streets, as if just listening to them is encouraging and abetting crime. Father Hattie knows many of them by name and has heard their stories. He speaks for Africa's street children to donor groups in Europe and North America who want to be in solidarity with them.

Father Hattie has witnessed the cruel mistreatment of street children by the authorities. He has observed how the police have confiscated the boys' few collected belongings and he has been told repeatedly by the girls of unscrupulous members within the police force who routinely demand sexual favors. The girls oblige out of fear. Once he observed a police officer dragging a mentally handicapped street child by his foot through the street with his head smashing repeatedly against the ground. Father Hattie ordered the officer to stop. Getting nowhere, the priest had to strike the officer with an umbrella before he would stop. When asked to explain his actions, the officer fled without the child.

Perhaps the ultimate abdication of moral responsibility toward the street children of Kampala took place when President Bill Clinton and his family visited the city. Clinton was the first sitting American president to visit Uganda. Before he arrived, hundreds of street children were rounded up and thrown into prison so that the nation's prominent visitors would not be subjected to any eyesores. The sentiment of the day was that the national scourge had to be removed from the streets, no matter how. The children were imprisoned and kept out of sight until after the Clintons had left the country.

As I walked though the city with Father Hattie, I noticed how the children's eyes light up with the look of recognition and friendship when they first see him approaching. He doesn't give them food or money. He does, however, find his own way to build a bridge of trust to them. I gradually came to understand that Father Hattie has something very valuable to offer these children, something they are living without—the kind of presence you are likely to find in a very loving home. He cares about these youngsters and their future, and it shows. He tells me: "At times it almost brings tears to my eyes when I see one of these children taking a small banana a tourist has given him and breaking it into six or seven pieces to share. These kids will pass around an ice cream cone or bottle of Coca Cola so each can have a lick or sip, or they will share an old newspaper or torn piece of plastic to use as a blanket on Kampala's streets."

Father Hattie has had remarkable success in inviting street children in Kampala to consider an alternative to life on the streets.

He has worked with Comboni priests and sisters to build homes that provide much of the stability of life and nurture that young people crave. The group's greatest success has been with the younger children. Father Hattie tells me it is crucial to get the children off the streets before substance abuse gains a lethal inroad into their young lives. The most pervasive and powerfully destructive temptation facing homeless young people is to cushion the pain of life on the streets with drugs.

Walking through Kampala's streets I observed many of the street kids huddled together in small groups, holding a piece of cloth to their nose. Father Hattie explained to me that nearly all the street children he has dealt with sniff *mafuta*, which is the local name for a form of kerosene. They keep a small bottle of *mafuta* in their pocket and a handkerchief or small rag on which they sprinkle the liquid. *Mafuta* is used by both boys and girls and is popular among the very youngest of the children. It is readily available because the older street boys are very willing to sell it to the younger children at a relatively inexpensive price.

This form of escapism, this forbidden pleasure, has a stranglehold on their young lives. With reckless abandon they pursue the solace they say they find in this momentary pleasure. They cling to it as though it holds a value of some kind too important to pass by. In the chaos of life on the streets where nothing makes sense, there remains this instantaneous pleasure.

I asked a fourteen-year-old boy living on the streets of Kampala to help me understand what it is that draws him and his companions into using drugs. He was brutally honest: "I cannot survive on the streets without using drugs. There are different types of drugs that I normally use. I take marijuana, *mafuta*, glue, tobacco, *mairungi* (an herb that is chewed), and alcohol. These drugs give me relief and let me forget my worries and problems. They make me feel warm and strong. Others make me sharp and sensitive to danger. If I'm sick, they take away pain, and when I'm bored they give me some excitement." In other words, this youngster seeks in drugs the protection, joy, and companionship that most children find elsewhere, especially in the circle of a loving family.

Street children are at least minimally aware of the dangerous aspect of using drugs. The danger is hard to deny as they see the impaired judgment and bizarre and violent behavior caused by the drugs' effects on their friends. In Kampala the street children have their own slang for someone who has become completely unhinged as a result of drug-taking: they say he or she has gone *zollo*.

When they are feeling depressed, angry, or hopeless, drinking and drugging provide cheap painkillers. Drugs can provide a momentary feeling of relief, but sometimes the contrary is true and the children end up feeling even worse. Even though drugs and alcohol may remain their constant companions while on the streets, these young people blithely anticipate a future that does not include the streets or the drugs. The street children I have met all consider their drug use a temporary activity. Unfortunately, however, most become addicted, having misunderstood or underestimated the habituating force of the drugs and the permanent damage to their brain cells.

The most positive and hopeful experience I had while researching the plight of street children was to accompany Father Hattie and Comboni Sister Adalgesa to one of their homes for kids who have opted out of life on the streets. The home we visited was supervised by two young men, both former seminarians, whom all the children called "uncle." Forty-five boys, from five to fifteen years old, live together in a structure that is more suited for ten or twelve people. Happily, their new home is under construction. Nevertheless, they seem extremely content to have each other, three meals a day, access to education, and, best of all, "uncles" genuinely interested in their well-being, people on whom they can count.

The altruism of these two former seminarians is impressive. They work for practically no pay, viewing their commitment as a ministry, a chance to give back to God in gratitude for their own loving families. They want to be for these children what their parents were for them. The youngsters flock to them. They constantly wrap themselves around their uncles and bask in their attention. After gaining the children's trust, the uncles attempt to trace the whereabouts of the children's families and to learn what led to the family breakup. Oftentimes the children deliberately give misinformation because they are very content here and have no desire to leave. Life in their new home is for some of them the only positive experience of family they have ever known. This seems to motivate the uncles to create an optimal experience for those entrusted to their care. The boys obey the uncles unquestioningly and are extremely respectful.

As Sister Adalgesa handed out the small candies she had brought, she smiled at each child. I was struck how a few children, after unwrapping the candy, put the wrapper in their pockets. They sucked on the candy for a few minutes and then returned it safely to its wrapping so it could be enjoyed again later, prolonging the fun. In the end, the children would keep the foil wrappers too and make little ornaments out of them. There is literally nothing that is wasted or thrown away in this house.

I sensed that small kindnesses like those of Sister Adalgesa go a long way in communicating to these kids that, indeed, they are prized by others and that there are people who delight in their happiness. This is a treasure not readily found on the streets.

That afternoon I met Deogratias. This fourteen-year-old boy was elated to be in his new situation after several unhappy years of living on the streets of Kampala and sleeping on the tarmac. He had been born into a family of twelve children, ten girls and two boys. With sadness in his voice he told me how his mother had simply walked out of their village home one day and never returned. He blames his father, who routinely beat her and the children. Deogratias added that the police in Kampala had beaten him with just as much force. Since his father did not have enough money for school fees and meals for his children, Deogratias decided to strike out on his own. He never experimented with *mafuta* or other drugs. This is so unusual that the street kids have a slang word for those who never take drugs: they are called *bafalla*. Seeing how happy Deogratias has become in the protection of people who care deeply for him fills me with awe at the transforming power of love.

Today, by God's grace and human ingenuity, more than half the children befriended by Father Hattie attend school. Still others are learning the skills of carpentry, tailoring, and brick-making. They sense that a future lies ahead for them.

There are more than two hundred million homeless children who walk the streets of our cities and villages across the globe. They have no homes or loving families to return to at the end of the day. The children I met in Uganda were playful, fun-loving, and, of course, very self-reliant for their age. They also share a terrible curse: each one feels fundamentally alone in the world. They often hang out in small groups during the day and at night they sleep huddled together, their bodies intertwined for protection. Each of these youngsters has known the terrible pain that accompanies those whom no one claims as their own.

The next time you find yourself driving or walking in a large city, open your eyes and look around you. Whether the city is in Latin America, the United States, Uganda or Tanzania, India or Hong Kong, you'll see unloved and unwanted youngsters asking to be noticed, asking for a space at the table. It's time to stop looking away. It's time to stop pretending we don't see them. It's time to rethink our responses, to smile, and to take action.

Epilogue

C hildren are always learning. They are unstoppable. Learning is part of their very nature. What they learn, however, depends on the actions of the adults around them. This truth became compellingly clear to me as I listened to a former child soldier in the Great Lakes region of Africa. This teenager related, "I did learn some things when I was with the rebels. I learned how to shoot, how to lay anti-personnel mines, and how to live on the run. I was taught how to use an AK-47 12-inch, which I could dismantle in less than one minute. When I turned twelve, they gave me an RPG [rocket-propelled grenade], because I had proved myself in battle."

I recoiled when I heard his words, unable at first to accept that any child would be schooled in the ways of killing. But this young boy had been efficiently trained in how to kill; there was no denying the truth of his statement. The sad and grim truth is that humanity has often been exceedingly hostile to its own children.

As small children rummage through garbage heaps for a scrap of food to eat, each of us should be ashamed of the world we have created for them. In times of armed conflict and civil unrest, as well as in times of famine and desperation, young girls, and sometimes boys, are forced to exchange sex for food, shelter, protection, identification papers, and all those things without which it is impossible to live. Is this a world we can be proud of and want to pass on to the next generation?

As children in Asia and Africa watch their parents die for lack of anti-retroviral therapies and other life-saving medicines, adults in North America are bombarded with television commercials

Henry/Maryknoll

Poverty cannot hide the dignity and innocence
of this Peruvian child.

reminding them that they can ill afford to live without the blissful effects of drugs like Viagra. During this past decade, according to UNICEF, there has been a "global undeclared war" on women, children, and adolescents. In 2003 the United States Congress passed substantial tax cuts for the nation's economic elite, while education for the nation's most vulnerable children remains precariously insecure. In Central America, children as young as nine or ten feel lucky when they get the chance to make some money laboring to the point of exhaustion in filthy sweatshops. Each of us is forced to ask: "Are we sabotaging our own future?"

There is a natural childhood innocence that shines in the eyes of young boys and girls. Yet, for millions of children who are not gifted with nurture, who are abandoned or mistreated by the adult world that surrounds them, there is no innocence. Instead, their eyes are clouded by fear and deep mistrust. What do these sad, bewildered looks tell us about ourselves and about the moral foundations of the society we are building?

A fundamental moral measure of any society is how its youngest and most vulnerable members fare. As we look at our own nation, we must ask: Why is it that the younger you are in the United States, the more likely you are to be poor? Indeed, nearly 20 percent of our preschool children are growing up poor in a land of plenty. We have failed to fully acknowledge that the lives of our children are the truest indicators of the strength and future vitality of our communities.

What is true of our nation is true of our world. For the human family to reclaim its soul, our most urgent priority must be the plight of vulnerable children.

Our children want to live in a world at peace. Those who dream of peace have a deep sense of our shared humanity. Those who build peace recognize the visible and invisible bonds that link us to every other person. Peace-loving people understand that their identity is in some mysterious way bound up with their fellow human companions, with their lives and their destiny. Children are often the first to see and embrace all the wondrous ties that knit the human family together. If more adults were to look around our

world with the eyes of children, that world would be a safer and
more gentle place.

All of us need to remember that Jesus responded to the question "Who is my neighbor?" with the story of a man whom history
calls the "Good Samaritan." Unlike the others before him, this
man stopped and ministered to a person lying helpless in a ditch.
He sensed the silent appeal on the face of the other, the desperate
look that said, "I can live if you are on my side."

I wonder why we do not have eyes to see that same look on
the faces of the millions of children in our world today, children
who need the basic necessities of life—a safe neighborhood in
which to grow up, a good education, access to health care, someone to love and protect them.

Jesus of Nazareth lies hidden and helpless in all of humanity's
most vulnerable children, those for whom there is no room at the
table. May we know the grace of our loving God in them and rebuild our troubled world for them to enjoy as God's beloved
daughters and sons.

Acts of Solidarity with Children: Observe, Judge, Act

Through the stories of the children chronicled on these pages, the cruelty of hunger, disease, violence, gender bias, and sexual exploitation is revealed as an unremitting enemy that overpowers millions of young people. We need to open our eyes to this and make a moral judgment, recognizing that what we are witnessing is completely unworthy of the nobility the Creator intends for each son and daughter of God. To act on behalf of the weakest and youngest members of the human family is simply to give flesh to God's own desires for human living.

The following are acts of solidarity, actions that we can take in the name of the love we owe one another as sisters and brothers.

1. Find a globe or world map; let your finger rest on a particular country and spend a few minutes in prayer for the children of that country. This could be a daily or weekly practice.

2. McDonald's offers "Happy Meals" for children. Find out how much a Happy Meal costs in your area and once a week put aside that amount. Choose the date of your own birthday, your celebration of life, to send a check for the accumulated amount to Catholic Relief Services with the proviso that this donation provide "food for children"—a "Happy Meal." (Catholic Relief Services, P.O. Box 17090, Baltimore MD 21203-7090; 1-800-736-3647; or on the web at www.catholicrelief.org)

3. Multicultural education is necessary for all children. Visit the children's section of your local bookstore. Purchase a storybook about children from another country, preferably a third-world country. Donate it to your parish school or religious education program or parish or local library.

4. Impressionable children take their cues from the adult world around them. When you are in the company of children, be mindful of acting compassionately and for the good of others. What you do for others not only creates greater solidarity in the human family but also witnesses to our young that we all belong to one another.

5. For the forty days of Lent each year, look at your world through the eyes of a vulnerable child, one who simply craves protective love. Remember that this is what all humanity seeks—to be held safe in the security that love alone can provide.

6. Identify programs for children in your community (parish, library, schools, community center) and volunteer your services.

7. Inform yourself about children's needs by placing your name on the mailing list of an organization that supports children's needs, such as UNICEF, UNESCO, the International Red Cross, Amnesty International, International Save the Children Alliance, Defence for Children International, the Global Network of Religions for Children. Most of these organizations have websites with contact information.

Peace for the Children of God

O God, all holy one,
you are our Mother and our Father,
and we are your children.
Open our eyes and our hearts
so that we may be able to discern
your work in the universe
and be able to see your features
in every one of your children.
May we learn that there are many paths
but all lead to you.
Help us to know that you have created us
for family, for togetherness,
for peace, for gentleness,
for compassion, for caring, for sharing.

May we know that you want us
to care for one another
as those who know
that they are sisters and brothers,
members of the same family,
your family,
the human family.

Help us to beat our swords into plowshares
and our spears into pruning hooks,
so that we may be able to live
in peace and harmony,
wiping away the tears
from the eyes of those
who are less fortunate than ourselves.
And may we know war no more,
as we strive to be
what you want us to be:
your children. Amen.

Desmond M. Tutu, Archbishop Emeritus of Cape Town, South Africa
(From the Education for Justice website of the Center of Concern)